KEEPING YOUR A!

KEEPING YOUR A!

*Motivating Our Children
to Higher Altitudes*

Chana R. Thompson-Brooks

XULON PRESS

Xulon Press
2301 Lucien Way #415
Maitland, FL 32751
407.339.4217
www.xulonpress.com

Unless otherwise indicated, Scripture quotations taken from the King James Version (KJV) –*public domain.*

Printed in the United States of America.

Paperback ISBN-13: 978-1-6628-0850-0
eBook ISBN-13: 978-1-6628-0851-7

Inspired by my angels, Sharia M. Webb
and Drew A. Thompson

Dedicated to my children Elliott, II and Elese Brooks.
Thank you for making Mommy a better me!

To my parents Karen Hughes, and Grady and Rhonda
Thompson, thank you for your unconditional love and
support. Thank you for loving me so much. It is because
of you all, that I know how to love unconditional. I love
you all soooooo much!

To Elliott G. Brooks, Sr., thank you for being on this
parenthood journey with me.

To my sisters Kendre, Deanna, Sharia, Sheila and Barbara,
the definition of sisterhood started with us.

To my ride or dies, Torsha, Shalese, Nina, Danielle, Rose,
Yolanda, Nashonda, Iris, Debbie, Pamela, and Trina Thank
you, Thank you, Thank you! You all are my rocks when
I need it!

To my pastor, Dr. Brodie I. Johnson of Cornerstone
Institutional Baptist Church, thank you for your prayers,
teaching and brotherly guidance.

To my sorority sisters of Iota Phi Lambda Sorority, Inc. –
Zeta Delta Chapter- thank you for polishing me
and helping me keep my crown straight.

Finally, to CT, thank you for who you are in my life. Past,
present and future, you bring out better me. You know my
innermost thoughts and feelings and don't judge. When I
pray, you pray. When I am off my game, you surely know
how to lift me up. Listening and learning from you, brings
clarity. Thank you. I love you and me very much.!

INTRODUCTION

When my youngest sister Sharia passed away in 2007, my world completely changed. I began looking at life completely different. She was a true inspiration to me. She took life by its wings and flew to new heights. Before her passing, she understood my desire to be a leader and mentor for others. You see, I have always had the desire to create or own something that will allow me to leave a legacy for my children. Sharia and I had many discussions about all types of things- life, love, happiness, education, dreams, goals and the list goes on. Knowing that I had a passion for young people, I wanted to use my skills and talents to educate and mentor children. Sharia shared the idea of "MOCHA (Motivating Our Children to Higher Altitudes)!" MOCHA represents the melting pot of all children. It represents how we can mentor and love on all children!" This conversation has always stuck with me.

Moving through life, I have picked up a few life lessons. These lessons that have taught me a lot- some good and some bad. My Uncle Drew would always say to me "Baby girl, you got to keep your A!" We are born with the grade of A. It is up to us to keep it! You keep it by being obedient, loving, kind, and a blessing to others. God is our teacher and he is grading your efforts to make him proud.

Praying for my children daily is as easy as a Sunday morning. When Elliott and Elese were little, I was blessed to take them to work with me. Every morning we would stand in my office and pray. I would pray for their days and attitudes (especially that little girl people Elese. She was something fierce). It got so good to them that Elliott would run to the office and ready himself to pray before I made it there. He would gather his little self and lead that thing ya'll! This was our normal. When they grew older and into middle and high school, I began traveling across the country for work. As I began traveling, daily prayer became more and more important. I had to stay connected to my children. I realized that not only did I have to keep my A but I was responsible for equipping my children, Elliott and Elese with the tools they need to keep their A. It is something to see that your children know God and know how to seek him for themselves. So, the journey of this book began!

It began as simple daily motivations and prayers for my children that I posted to their Facebook pages each morning in my absence (That I knew they would check!). But then it evolved. My family and friends began to see the words and looked forward to them each day (and would get an attitude if they were not there). That's when God gave me the confirmation I needed. I am forever grateful for this assignment of God and I am willing to accept it. I now truly understand the power of prayer. I am watching my children be blessed. My children know God for themselves and seek him on their own. It is a wonderful thing to see and know that God is embedded in the fabric of their being. I pray that all that read this book are encouraged and willing to share it with some special "Love bug" in your life. It works for everyone! Be blessed good people.

Best,
Chana

GOD'S TOUCH

Burlington, VT is absolutely BEAUTIFUL!! As I opened my eyes this morning, I looked out on to Lake Champlain and thought I am in the presence of God. I thought this is a great place to unplug and escape from the world. As I have moved throughout my time here, I have noticed all of God's little touches. Sometimes when we are in the hustle and bustle of busy everyday life, it is refreshing to be surrounded by relaxation. Anybody who knows me understands that I am a very reflective person and use my own personal reflections to drive my success. I don't need anyone to tell me my weaknesses. (Lord, knows I have them!) I can clearly articulate them myself but, my solace is knowing that I have God's touch to guide me. It is the small details that make events in our lives grand. I love experiencing God's little touches or reminders each day. (They sholl make me feel good!) I challenge you to look for God today!

Lord today, I thank you for the touches and reminders each day that you indeed exist! Thank you for the details. You created this world and so eloquently place your presence. Let us stop and take notice! Lord, I appreciate you for allowing us to be in awe of you. As Elliott Brooks and Elese Brooks travel throughout this day, show them your presence. Guide them and remind them that you are God and God all by yourself. I ask this in your son Jesus name, Amen!

Be blessed good people!

PROBLEM FIXER

I am being very transparent this morning. I struggle with perfection! I am a planner, and all things have to be just so. When my plans go awry, I get a little agitated. Problem solver mode then kicks in. In my little brain, I have programmed myself to fix all that is broken. But you know the older I get and the wiser I get, I realize that somethings just have to stay broken. Somethings are not my responsibility to fix. Things that are not in my control I have to let be. AND it's OK! (Wow, big revelation for me!) As I was reading Sarah Young this morning, I said: "God you sent that confirmation swiftly!!!" She said, and I quote "You tend to go into problem-solving mode all too readily, acting as if you have the capacity to fix everything. This is a habitual response, so automatic that it bypasses your conscious thinking. Not only does this habit frustrate you, but it also distances you from Me." Baby if that ain't me! Now, I may be the best Mommy and wife; I may have the bomb resume, I may know the right people, I may even be good at all that I do. But God, I am not!!!! We are so limited in our abilities to fix things in our lives! Every time we think that we have fixed a problem or issue, know God is indeed the fixer. Let's place him 1st!

Lord, I thank you. Thank you for revelation! In my spirit God, I feel you! Allow us to listen to you, put you 1st! Problems will come, but God you are the fixer. Remove all adversity. Lord, today! Bless my children, Elliott Brooks and Elese Brooks. If they are experiencing problems unknown, be their fixer. I ask this in your son Jesus name, Amen!

TOTAL VICTORY

Today is a good day. (It's my birthday!) I do a lot of self-reflecting during this time. I want to see how far I have grown, what I have accomplished, where I have fallen short, what I need to work on, how I am balancing life, what choices I need to make, etc... Most times, I surprise myself as I conduct my yearly review. This year is a little different. Yes, I have accomplished some things, but I have failed at things as well (complete transparency - I really sucked at some things). But I can tell you all this, I feel God all over me. I feel him elevating me to something new and different! I have always said, "This life as I know it can't be all that God has for me!" God has plans for you and me. We have to: 1.) want it, 2.) receive it, and 3.) believe and trust Him. You see he wants to give us the desires of our hearts, but we have to work at it. Unless you achieve total victory, you feel defeated, but your total victory may not be the victory God wants out of the situation. As I begin this new year of life, I am going to be a new Chana! Learning to let go of fears, normalcy, and achieving God's total victory.

Father God, how you doing? I am thankful for you and your movement in my life! You are awesome and deserve all the glory and honor. You sholl know how to humble a sista! And I thank you! Thank you for humility, peace, and victory! Lord let you shine through my life. This year, Lord make it anew. Renew my faith and trust in you! Difficulty and disappointment may come, but God let me see them as preparation for your next level! I am ready Lord! Bless my children, Elliott Brooks and Elese Brooks. Allow them to receive all that you have for them! I ask this in your son Jesus name, Amen!

Be blessed good people!

ASSIGNMENT

A task or piece of work assigned to someone as part of a job or course of study. As I sat this morning listening to Jameliah Young-Mitchell speak about a virtuous woman, I thought about that thing y'all. I began to think about the assignments God gives us. Ask yourself, how many of you really follow God's will and plan for your life? We sometimes take our assignment from God and turn it into more than just that-an assignment. We take that assignment and turn it into our life's work. But sometimes (ya'll better get this) what you think is your life is only an assignment! When you were in school, teachers taught the lesson and then gave you the assignment to ensure you caught what was being taught. This was to test your knowledge and skills. This assignment then was used to build on to the next lesson. Like the teacher, God's assignments are designed to build on the next lesson. You can't move to your next level if you are stuck on the present assignment! MOVE Y'ALL!! Get unstuck! Ladies, you know when we get that piece of gum stuck to our heels, and it becomes a hot, sticky, mess. What do we do? We scrape it off! (We will look for the roughest piece of concrete we can find to get that mess off!) Scrape off your uncertainty, disappointments, and fears of moving to the next assignment and trust God! He never fails!

Father God, intercede right now Lord. Show us our next assignment. Give us the courage to stand for you and trust you! Lord today reign down your assignments for us! Open our hearts and minds to receive them. Father, I ask that today as my children Elliott Brooks and Elese Brooks read this message, they too receive their assignment and lesson from you. Bless today. In your son Jesus name, Amen! Be blessed good people!

CLEAR OUT

Daylight savings time just happened this past weekend. We have become accustomed to certain rituals when that happens such as things, like changing the batteries in the smoke detectors, servicing the fire extinguisher, switching your summer clothes for fall and winter clothes (Y'all know I love me some Fall!!!! True New Yorker!), Spring and Fall deep cleaning. However, for me, it is times like these that I also do deep self-reflections of where I am in life. Am I where I want to be spiritually, professionally, as a mom, wife, daughter, sister, friend, etc. That's interesting thought, huh? Sarah Young in the book *Jesus Calling* states "My main work is to clear out debris and clutter, making room for My Spirit to take full possession." Isn't it a beautiful thing to know that God gives us that ability to connect with him? Today, I feel so blessed! Blessed and ready to do the work that God has for me to do! I say to you clean out and see your way clear! God has a purpose!

Father God today, help us clear out and welcome you into our lives! Show us what you have for us to do! I ask that you give each of us a clear vision of what you have in store for our lives. Protect our minds, bodies, and souls. Remain, constant Lord. As my babies, Elliott Brooks and Elese Brooks start their day show them their clear purpose. I ask this in your son Jesus name, Amen!

Be blessed good people!

KINGDOM BUILDING

Obedience. Traveling home last week Friday after a long day at work, sitting on the plane I wondered, "What's next Lord?" Having a hard day at work, I wanted to be depressed and wallow in my self-pity, but my spirit wouldn't let me (For too long anyway). I walked in the house and just wanted to be. But you know when God has a plan for you. At that moment, I asked God for confirmation. I needed and yearned for him to confirm my path. On Saturday, I went to our church banquet. (We clean up nicely y'all. We were sugar sharp!!) I was all dolled up but feeling a little downtrodden. As I set there feeling the hell from the week, having to welcome God's people and give praise to our fearless pastor, I am feeling spiritually weak. But I'm telling you GOD moves swiftly y'all. As I took my seat in obedience to the kingdom work, God said "Listen little one, I am here, and your situation is about to change, I have work for you to do! Now with your cute self, watch me work!" It was if God said "Listen Pastor Martin my child is weak and disappointed right now. Here's what I want you to tell her..." Baby, when I left there, confirmation, was given!!! God has to transition you and position you for your transformation!!! I received that word!!! You see that's why God wouldn't let those tears flow, that anger to fester, those ungodly words to utter out my mouth. He was positioning me to focus on the task and the vision he has for me!!! Lord knows I am ready for my next level. What about you?

Lord today as I sit here, I praise you! I thank you for disappointment. Disappointment allows me to focus on you! What a blessing. Lord thank you for minor setbacks. Let us use them to gain major opportunities. You are so awesome. I love how you work God! Your keen eye and righteous spirit are what we need daily. Lord, I thank you. Thank you for swift moving. I thank you for my children Elliott Brooks and Elese Brooks. All I do is for you and them. Continue to move in my life. I ask in your son, Jesus name, Amen.

This was for me today! Be blessed good people!

REFRAME AND REFOCUS

Today I awoke at my regular, 5:32 am time. (That's my time with God y'all.) But today was a little different. As soon as my eyes open, I expected the same ritual. That didn't happen. My mind was all over the place. (Doesn't surprise me. I can be a little scatter brained at times, lol) As I started praying and meditating, I started drifting to other to do list things- work meetings, customer issues, travel schedule, etc. I had to ask God to still my mind and REFOCUS me! You see all those little things that had me unfocused on him needed to REFRAMED to opportunities for good instead of nagging issues. Let me show you how quickly God works. Just as I asked him to still my mind, I began reading my daily devotional, and it spoke on this- "It is often these minor setbacks that draw you away from My Presence. When you reframe setbacks as opportunities, you find that you gain much more than you have lost." Isn't God good? This is why I love him! He is always on time. So today good people, refocus and reframe. God is an on time God! For those of you who don't know- Today is a good day!

Thank you, God, for your on time wisdom! I thank you for stilling my mind today to focus on you! When life fails us, people steal our joy, love ones leave us, finances are low, children are crazy, friends forsake us, and the world overtakes us, you are right there! Right there all the time! Today show your sovereign swiftness. Change lives today! As Elliott Brooks and Elese Brooks start their day today, reframe their disappointments to opportunities. I ask this in your son Jesus name, Amen!

Be blessed good people!

SPIRIT

How befitting on the Hallelujahween! (Thank you, God, for the inspiration.) How many of you remember when cheerleader squads were called "The Spirit Team"? This team brings the spirit to the sports games, pep rallies, and other events. Their job is to breathe life into a situation. I remember being on our spirit team in high school - "Greg Evans, 69 if he can't do it no one can!" (Seneca Class of 1991) My sister's better half calls me "Spirit"! (I wonder why. I think it's his way of saying I am a bit much! Lol) But in any case, I take it as a compliment! When life beats you down, God and the Holy Spirit breathes life into you. If you are open to receive, watch how He can change a situation. Pray for the spirit of God to breathe into your life today.

So today as the little ones are out this evening gathering their treats, be careful and safe! Prayers going up today.

Father God, thank you for your spirit! Spread it today. Remove evilness, wrongdoing, and people with ill intent. Today as my children Elliott Brooks and Elese Brooks start their day, breath your spirit into them. In your son Jesus name, Amen!

Be blessed good people!

SAY YEAH, YEAH, YEAH

This word means "yes." But did you know that its first use was in 1863? Now it is used more than the actual word yes! Listening to "Just Want to be Happy" by Kirk Franklin, one course says "Say yeah, yeah, yeah!" (I would sing for you, but you would say "No, no, no!) This entire song ministers about being happy and how to get there. Simply put you have to say Yeah! Yeah to being happy, saved, loved, peaceful, and wanted. Get one of those deep belly groans and scream YEAH! (Y'all know how that loud church lady yells out in church!) Let Jesus handle the naysayers. When your husband or wife is crazy, say YEAH! When your job is crazy, or you don't have one, say YEAH! When your children don't act as they should, say YEAH! When any adversaries come your way, say YEAH! God is filled with many YEAHS! He is waiting to fill you up. Go through today just saying YEAH, YEAH, YEAH! People may think you're a little special, but when you think of the goodness of Jesus and the many things God is waiting to say Yeah to, you won't care! When they are looking, say " if you only knew what this Yeah is for, you will be trying to out Yeah me!"

God thank you for the YEAHS! Lord for those of us that are running on low fuel say YEAH! As we begin to move throughout the day, send gentle reminders that this world and all that is in it belongs to you! You say YEAH! Today as my children Elliott Brooks and Elese Brooks start their day, say YEAH! YEAH to what is right! I ask in your son Jesus name, Amen!

Be blessed good people!

ROLL, DIP, AND DRIP

S ounds like a course to a ratchet song or steps to one of
these crazy dances the kids are doing these days (looking
like they are having convulsions, seizures, or strokes) in essence
are instructions. In either case, it is something we follow or
internalize. On Sunday, my pastor preached "I Have Reached
My Turning Point! Hmmmm (That's all I have to say on
that.) Some of us are "wallowing." Wallow means to roll oneself about in a lazy, relaxed, or ungainly manner; to become or
remain helpless; to indulge oneself immoderately. We wallow
in our circumstances or situations- our un-pleasantries. Nine
times out of ten these were of our own doing. But what God is
saying to us is Roll, Dip, and Drip! Roll over your situation to
Him, Dip in his presence, and Drip in his love. Stop wallowing
and become a "WALLOWER"! You see wallow also has a
second set of meanings -to devote oneself entirely; especially
to take unrestrained pleasure; to become abundantly supplied.
God has an all call out for WALLOWERS! Will you audition?
Here the requirements:

1. Love God and Yourself
2. Be willing to Roll, Dip and Drip
3. Have an open mind and heart for different

If you meet these qualifications, call Him, he is waiting!

Father God, I thank you today. Thank you for this incred-
ible opportunity you have given me to be a blessing to others.
With every stroke of my finger, I bless myself. Lord let all that
read these see you and the sincerity! Lord open people's heart
and minds to different. Send calming spirits. Today Lord look

on my children Elliott Brooks and Elese Brooks. Allow them to Roll, Dip, and Drip. But also, today Lord to the same for me! I ask in your son Jesus name, Amen!

Roll, Dip, and Drip!
Roll, Dip, and Drip!
Roll, Dip, and Drip!
Be blessed good people!

HAPPY SHARIA "BABY" DAY!

Today I woke up out of a crazy dream. I was dreaming about a "Baby" that I found. In a nutshell, the dream involved a baby and shooting. (Child, that was some crazy mess!) I jump out of my sleep to get out that craziness. I immediately began to pray. Then I looked up what this dream signifies. If you dream that the baby is smiling at you, then it suggests that you are experiencing pure joy. You do not ask for much to make you happy. If you find a baby in your dream, then it suggests that you have acknowledged your hidden potential. Alternatively, forgetting about a baby represents an aspect of yourself that you have abandoned or put aside due to life's changing circumstances. The dream may serve as a reminder that it is time for you to pick up that old interest, hobby, or project again. To see a shooting in your dream indicates that you have a set goal and know what to aim for in life. Your plans are right on target! How befitting! As we celebrate Sharia day, let's be reminded with "Baby" love, of the pure joy we have in our lives. People, it is the small things that make us happy. I encourage you today to find what makes you happy. Live again! Reflect on the most joyous moments in your life! Free yourself of your past! Shoot for those unreachable dreams. Know that "Baby" is that guardian angel watching over us today! Brooks loves you "Baby"!

Lord thank for clarity today! Today encourage others to experience PURE JOY!! I can't thank you enough for pure joy!!! Joy in knowing that we can grow pass hurt, anger, sorrow and strife. Comfort in knowing the pain and suffering doesn't last forever. But PURE JOY is with you! Today as we celebrate the "Baby," thank you for reassuring us that we all have something to be happy about! Allow my children, Elliott Brooks and Elese Brooks, to experience "Baby" love! In your son Jesus name, Amen! Happy Sharia Day!!! Be blessed good people.

LOVE IS IN THE AIR

Such a cliche! Just a food for thought "Why does it take one day to signify your love for someone?" Love has no limits and should be celebrated every day! Loving someone and showing them love is an act that needs no perimeters! Ladies let's try this: Let's get so lost in love with God that guy has to seek Him to find you! Now that's love!!! Men why not show love the way God designed it to be? Proverbs 18:22 " He who finds a wife finds a good thing and obtains favor from the LORD." The keyword here is HE. Sometimes we want to be found so badly that we lose our mind!! When a man finds his good thing, he is also adequately prepared by God to fulfill his role!

I am not here to be Sister Dream Slayer (Ladies let those men love on you today!) I am here to tell you that your love is worthy of more than a raggedy dying rose, a cheap balloon and that nasty box of candy that you never eat! Love, learn, and trust God together!

Lord thank you for sincere LOVE! Your love is unchanging and everlasting. All this prompt and circumstance will fade, but you are always right there! Today as my children Elliott Brooks and Elese Brooks start this day, let them know the unwavering love that I have for them! Let the love you have for them shine today! I ask this in your son Jesus name, Amen!

Love hard and be blessed, good people!

VISION

As we move through life having direction is so important. Part of direction is a vision. Have you ever noticed that in every aspect of your life there is an overarching vision? At school, the teachers and administrators provide their vision for their students. At work, companies have a vision. At home, parents have a vision for their children. I remember after each birth of my children, I prayed over and with them. My prayer was two-fold. I asked God to equip me to be the parent he expected me to be. (Child, my mind was bad!) I asked that he keep them covered. I asked that they know God for themselves. But most of all, I prayed that he provided me a VISION for their lives. No surprise to me, God sent me back to his word, Habakkuk 2:2-3 "And the Lord answered me, and said, Write the vision, and make it plain upon tables, that he may run that readeth it. For the vision is yet for an appointed time, but at the end, it shall speak, and not lie: though it tarry, wait for it; because it will surely come, it will not tarry." I was watching Steve Harvey (Y'all know that's my man crush.) He was speaking about vision boards. He referenced these verses. However, what he failed to mention is what Habakkuk did in verse 1. He stood at his watchtower and waited to hear from God. I don't know about you, but what this said to me was Habakkuk was like "Looka here God, I am about to go in this here closet, sit, pray, and wait for you to show me something!" Habakkuk knew this was too much for him!

When God gives you direction and a vision, you can rest assured that he is going to equip you to carry it out. Pray, write, make it clear, and watch God work!

Father God, thank you for the vision. God as I sit back and look back over the years, you have done just as you promised! I asked and you sure delivered! THANK YOU, GOD! Thank you for the humbleness in my son Elliott Brooks. Thank you for the caring spirit in my daughter Elese Brooks. No, they are not perfect, but they make me proud every day! Lord thank you for the visions you have assigned me. I ask that you continue to walk with me on this journey! I ask this in your son Jesus name, Amen,

Be blessed good people!

UP IN HERE

In June 2000, DMX released a song called Party Up! (I was good and pregnant with one of my boolicious babies, Elliott Brooks.)

"Y'all gon' make me lose my mind
Up in here, up in here!
Y'all gon' make me go all out
Up in here, up in here!
Y'all gon' make me act a FOOL
Up in here, up in here!
Y'all gon' make me lose my cool

Up in here, up in here!" Y'all remember. (I bet some of you are bobbing right now to it in your head! lol)

Just as this song pumps you up, so should God. When you sit and think of all the things that God has done for you, (as my pastor said on Sunday) "Sometimes you just want to HOLLER up in here!" You see, we focus on the big blessings and miracles that God does. But oh, he does so many more small things that we take for granted and overlook!

Here's my transparent moment: I struggle with being still! (For my entire family, I finally admit it- I am a busy body!) Sitting still can sometimes be uncomfortable for me. It makes me face some hard truths! It brings clarity, focus, and perspective! Oh but when all is clear, I want to HOLLER up in here!! Holler because I receive the blessing, lesson, and story that God wants me to share! (There is a process to these FB post.) Just this morning I had to apologize to God while I was praying because my mind was wandering in the mist of my prayer. And in an instant, God gave me confirmation. I opened my devotional and the message today said "IT'S ALL RIGHT TO BE HUMAN. When your mind wanders while you are praying, don't be surprised or upset. Simply return your attention to Me. Share a secret smile with Me, knowing that I understand." Baby, I wanted to holler but at 5:00 am, I think I would have given my family a heart attack!

So here's my challenge to you today, find somewhere to holler today! It could be in your car, closet, kitchen, office, park. Take a moment to thank God for all he has done! When you have, hollered, reply to this post by saying "Hollered!"

Lord thank you for touching and agreeing. You said in your word Matthew 18:19 "Again I say unto you, That if two of you shall agree on earth as touching anything that they shall ask, it shall be done for them of my Father which is in heaven." We are being obedient Lord expecting miracles and blessings today! God as Elliott Brooks and Elese Brooks start their day, make them want to holler! Holler because they are blessed. Father, I ask these things in your son Jesus name, Amen!

Be blessed good people!

THE 17TH

Today as I sat having breakfast with colleagues, I felt a beautiful peace come over me. A peace that you could almost smell and see. I then opened my itinerary for the day and there it was-January 17th. Now I know where that heavenly peace came from. Today as I sit quietly celebrating what would have been my youngest sister's 36th birthday, I am reminded of her passion! You see, your passion should always be greater than your fears. Sharia's passion for life, her determination, and zeal always overshadowed her fears that came along with her illness. She had a drive that most of us can only dream of having. So today, I challenge you to release your fears. Get out of your comfort zone. Follow your passion!

Father God, thank you! Lord, I praise you for desire, determination, and most of all passion. Lord, I ask that you continue to remove fear. Replace it with desire and the willingness to want better. As Elliott Brooks and Elese Brooks start their day today, remove fear. Help then to focus and determination. Show them that the sky is the limit. I ask this in your son, Jesus name, Amen!

Be blessed good people!

MOTIVATING NEEDS

Last week during a company meeting we discussed our personality index. The index includes "motivating needs" to which a manager can apply when supervising others. I am a firm believer that you treat people in a manner that is conducive to them. This got me to thinking about all of you love bugs! What motivates you? What are your motivating needs? If I can be completely transparent, I need a little attention every once and awhile. (Heck, I am sure you do too!) I don't need all the fanfare (Although my personality index says that I do...Hmmmm. Must be my alter eagle "Ms. Dafadill"!) Just enough to let me know you appreciate me, my work, my efforts, and determination. This could be as simple as saying "Good Job!" Having dinner the other night with my dad and stepmom (I hate that word by the way.) She acknowledged me by saying how good of a friend I am to the few that I have. That touched me because someone acknowledged something about me. (Thank you, Rhonda Thompson, for that.) Just that simple, my need was met. We all have needs that when met makes us feel good about ourselves. Having our needs met allows us to motivate others and as the old folks say "Go another further!" So in this year of happiness, find your motivating need and don't settle for not having it met. I guarantee you will feel better about yourself!

Father God, I just love your wisdom! I ask that you continue to fulfill all our needs! Continue to provide your loving touches to assure us that you are always near! Allow my children, Elliott Brooks and Elese Brooks, to discover their motivating needs. Give them all that their heart's desire. I ask this in your son Jesus name, Amen!

Be blessed good people!

FLU

As I sat this morning in the ER with my little love bug-Two, a mommy's natural instinct is to want to cradle her baby. (Y'all know Two is pitiful when he is sick!) I sat and watched helplessly as my baby was in pain, with chills, hot flashes, and vomiting. That hot mess of an FLU!!! As he rested, I began praying. You see I, FLU (First Looked Up)! The devil had no residency here! I asked God to heal his body as only he can! Happy to report he is finally at home resting well.

When all else fails, FLU-First Look Up! God knows what you are struggling with, battling, fighting off, and dealing with. Let prayer be your medicine, and God be your healing. Y'all check on my baby now!

Father God thank you for healing. Lord love on Elliott Brooks. Let him know that you can heal him with just one touch of your loving hand. Allow Elese Brooks and their dad the patience to care for Two in my absence. I ask in your son Jesus name, Amen.

Be blessed good people!

LET'S GO

And we are off! New year new start. As I sit here gazing at my new little niece, I thought wow she doesn't have a care in the world. She is new to this world. It is our responsibility to pour love, kindness, understanding, and knowledge into her. She will be as good as her world around her. Yes, she has wonderful parents and family that will ensure that she will be the best that she can be (her mom is a little cra-cra). They will equip her for success.

Now for us old seasoned fogeys, what will the new year bring you? Better yet what will you bring to the new year? Let me have a transparent moment: I am looking forward to a year of new and renewed!!!! Life is too short to waste! As faith would have it, I plan to embrace all that God has for me! Don't be surprised if I am a little selfish this year. God has a purpose and plan that he has assigned me, and I am working to accomplish His plan. More to come...

Father God thank you for wisdom. The wisdom to acknowledge you and seek your will. Lord as we embark on this new year, provide focus. Focus on you! Renew life, love, happiness, peace, and joy. Provide new opportunities, relationships, assignments, understanding, and kindness in the world. Lord as Elliott Brooks and Elese Brooks start the new year, mature them and focus them. I ask this in your son Jesus name, Amen! A year of HAPPINESS and FOCUS!

Be blessed good people!

THE END

As the year ends, a new chapter emerges. What will you tolerate in the new year? The key word is "NEW." When we bring in a new year, we always entertain new promises, ideas, resolutions, new love, new motivations, new, new, new. But what about the old? Have you cleaned out the old? Now don't get me wrong some old is wonderful (Chivalry never gets old!), but tradition has shown us that we should start new each year. Some of your decisions will not be popular and accepted by all. Happiness and hurt will occur. Choose happiness Y'all!!!!! Life is too short. I choose happiness. My happiness or your happiness may come at a cost. But know that God has it all under control! Walk into the new year with a purpose and plan. Whatever God has a place in your heart and spirit, step out on faith and do it! Now don't be crazy and jump without a plan and a prayer! (Y'all be running around here quitting jobs in the name of Jesus, and he will be saying "Fool when did I answer that prayer?") Here is what I suggest:

1. Pray and wait for clarity. Ask God to place it deep within your heart! You'll know you are making the right decision.
2. Get others out your ear and business. (Heck they have issues too.) Others aren't God!
3. Give it your best. Love hard and go hard. Give it all you got. And when it is all said and done, let God tell you that you did good and your assignment is complete! You can then move on in HAPPINESS! The best is yet to come!

Father God, thank you for last year and all it brought. The happy times, the losses, the defeats, the wins are what draws us closer to you! Lord, I pray that you send the best for your children! We need your covering. We need your blessings. We need your guidance. Open our hearts, minds, and ears to hearing you speak your desires for us. As the new year approaches, show my children Elliott Brooks and Elese Brooks just how strong and powerful you are. Focus me so that I can focus them! I ask this in your son Jesus name, Amen!

Be blessed good people!

IN CASE YOU DON'T
UNDERSTAND

Now that we have celebrated the life of my uncle, all family has returned to their prospective home, and life has resumed for us, I now find myself thinking about the reality of the situation. WOW!!!! Mind blowing!!!! As I sat watching and enjoying family at the repast, the finality hit me. He is actually gone. But not without one final joke! At his services during the most somber moment, the heaviness and sadness was broken by circus music! That's right you heard me - circus music! As I stood at the podium with my cousin, out of the blue my phone started playing this loud circus music. He showed us that there is humor in every situation. This set the tone for the rest of the service. We laughed and shared stories about our experiences with Uncle Drew. We were able to share memories and laughter through his slideshow. It turned out to be just what he wanted to be. (Short, sweet and to the point!!) But through it all, I surprised myself. IN CASE YOU DON'T UNDERSTAND...Strength and peace. God will give it to you. Everyone has been so gracious through this with Uncle Drewzy. I keep hearing God say to me Strength and peace...You know the funniest thing is just when you think you don't have it, God shows you that you do. You see sometimes we anticipate what we think is going to happen but honey let me tell you, God turns that thing around!!!! Let me say this to you, IN CASE YOU DON'T UNDERSTAND, God will give you the strength of an ant trying to carry food to the colony (Baby, them little things be working ya'll!) and peace that will have you to thinking you are crazy!!!!

Father God thank you for reflection! Time to reflect on your goodness. God as we go through our day, allow us to feel your presence and stop to acknowledge you! Allow us to share the IN CASE YOU DON'T UNDERSTAND moments today with those who don't know or understand the power of You. Lord as my children Elliott Brooks and Elese Brooks start their day, share with them strength and peace! Let them know without a shadow of a doubt, that you are real and always present. Provide peace and strength right now! In your son Jesus name, Amen!

Be blessed good people!

WHEN I FOUND OUT

In 1980, Diana Ross released a song, "Upside Down"...

I said upside down you're turning me
You're giving love instinctively
Around and round you're turning me
Upside down
Boy, you turn me
Inside out
And round and round
Upside down
Boy, you turn me
Inside out
And round and round

The realization of who God is, brings yummy a phenomenal feeling. I tell you what, just ask Him for a little taste. You will begin to see doors open, life changes, calm in the storm, unexplainable peace, insurmountable joy and good old grace and mercy. When I found out who He was for real, it turned my world UPSIDE DOWN! I don't mind being dizzy as long as it is dizzy for God! Sing on Diana!

Father God thank you for the dizziness. Being upside down for you is the best thing you can give to us. Lord, today I ask that you touch at least one person. Turn their world upside down. Bless my children Elliott Brooks and Elese Brooks today. Refocus their mind to you. Turn their world upside down! Bring out the best in them. I ask in your son Jesus name, Amen! Be blessed good people!

PRESERVING

To keep alive or in existence; make lasting. This morning I woke up and the word preserve was the first thing on my mind. As I began praying, God said " Difficulty may come but with me, we preserve that that is good!" As my family goes through this difficult loss, I never lose sight of God's plan. I was riding home last night with my boolicious son Elliott Brooks (Hey mommy's honey bun). As we talked about his Uncle Drew, he began to think and talk about all that they shared together. My response to him was, "Those are memories that you keep near and dear to your heart." Preserving... I spent many days and nights with my Uncle Drew trying to soak up wisdom (Yes, there was wisdom in his jokes. LOL), life lessons and laughter that I can pass along to those who will never get the chance to experience his presence. It has become clear to me how fortunate I am. I love all my uncles, but this one was special. Special because he listened, shared, laughed, and encouraged you to do the same. He touched all that he came in contact with. Today, I say PRESERVE! Preserve time with love ones, memories made, difficulty (because it's coming), love, happiness, and joy.

Father God thank you. Thank you for this day. Thank you for life, love and memories. I pray today for my family. Lord touch each of them. Show them that difficulty may come but God you are the keeper of difficulty. You seep into harden hearts, weeping souls, discouraged minds and restore love, peace, and joy. Lord, I know you will but as Drew is ushered into your kingdom, take care of our precious cargo. Allow him to rest in you know that all is well here on earth. Lord I thank you for allowing my children Elese Brooks and Elliott Brooks to experience this type of unconditional love. I ask in your son Jesus name, Amen!

Be blessed good people!!!

UNNECESSARY
AGGRAVATION

What I am learning in this life is that you only get one! One life to live to the fullest. Why should undo and unnecessary stress, aggravation, disappointment, fear, angry, worry, or strife be added to the mix? God does not give us the spirit of fear. Trusting and leaning on him is what he expects. So why should we not expect a stress-free life full of joy, peace, happiness, and certainty? I am learning that life is too short and precious to let the devil steal it away. We thank God for the struggles but let those struggles be lessons to brighter and greater things. My God is faithful and just!!

Father God, we thank you for precious gift of life!! Thank you for peace and joy! Lord I ask that you restore order in our homes, families, work, children, and friends. Send your anointing down on the world! We are living in perilous times. Times that only you can change. Lord I ask that Elliott Brooks and Elese Brooks never take for grant the blessings that you have provided them. I ask this in your son Jesus name, Amen.

Be blessed good people!

KEEPING YOUR A

From the moment we start school, we are taught the grading system. We learn that A is the best grade you can receive. This grading system now not only applies to school but to other things like restaurants, businesses, consumer products, etc... My Uncle Drew once told me you have to keep your A... What he said was that everyone is born with the grade of an A. It is up to us to keep it. You see, when we are created and come out the shoot (for those of you who need correct terminology- the womb) God gave us that perfect grade. The choices you make in life can cause you to keep it or lose a few points along the way. In his word, God equips us with all the tools and study guides we need to earn and keep our perfect gift from him. Where are you on the grading scale? If you are not on your A game, I suggest that you pull out your study guide - the Bible and get to it.

Father God thank you. Thank you for the book of knowledge that you have given us. Thank you for the wisdom you bestowed on us from the beginning. The word that you have passed to us. Bless my Uncle Drew as he travels along this path. Thank you for his 60th birthday! Restore his A... Show us how to keep our A. Bless my children Elliott Brooks and Elese Brooks. Teach them how to keep their A... In your son Jesus name, Amen.

Keep your A good people...

SPIT ON ME

I was working at my very first real job as a Pre-K teacher. I was so excited. I had my classroom decorated. Every student had their own place. My dad had come and built a loft in my classroom. I had brought a class turtle and rabbit. I was ready and prepared for the babies. Rearing to go, they rushed in one by one. They were super excited. But there was one. Oh, he was so beside himself. I placed him in a chair and got eye level with him and said "Baby you are going to be ok. They will be back." This child looked at me and SPIT! You already know I had to call Jesus quickly to remind me this this was a child and not my child. LOL! Instead of my initial reaction, I gathered him in my arms and held him and said, "It's ok, sweetheart!"

In this situation, we look at the spitting as something terrible! (And it is disgusting and can be belittling) A few week ago, my Pastor (Hey Dr. Brodie!) preached a sermon titled "I Can See Clearly Now." He talked about how Jesus spit on the blind man and he was made to see (Ya'll know the story. If not you need to get your bible and read!) The Spit!!! When Jesus spits on you, life changes, you change, people change, situations change! Spit is no longer disgusting. Baby you will be running around like a crackhead itching for that spit! (Oh, too much? I'm sorry) I encourage you today to ask God to spit on you.

Father God, good morning. Thank you for this day! Lord I ask today that you continue to spit life into us! Spit on situations and circumstances. Remove depression, pain, sorrow, agony and defeat. Replace these with your love and promises. Lord today watch over my family. Keep us moving Lord. In the mist of trouble, I know you are the author and finisher. Father today, I ask that you spit on my children Elliott Brooks and

Elese Brooks as they start their journey today. Show up today and be their blessing. I ask this today in your son Jesus name, Amen! Be blessed good people!

KNOWING YOUR
IMPORTANCE

Webster's dictionary defines importance as the state or fact of being of great significance or value. Sometimes we place ourselves in situations where we devalue our importance or worth. This could be at work, in relationships, friendships, or with family. As I was sitting in my office yesterday in my Bethesda office, I realized just how far God has brought me. I began thanking him for that. I start thinking-why me? Then I thought-why not me? You see when I asked why me, I was doubting my importance or worth. I realized that it is ok to recognize your value and worth and be confident (not cocky) about it. To know what you want, to have your expectations met, to stay true to yourself and not to settle for anything less may cause some discomfort and uncertainty. You may lose some people and things along the way. Loss is difficult but can be replaced greater rewards. Know that it is ok to ruffle a few feathers as long as you stay true to yourself. Know what battles to fight and which to let go. Life is too short to sell yourself short on your non-negotiables!

Father God thank you today for the revelation. Thank you for allowing me to know my importance and worth! Allow others to embrace their worth. Continue to build confidence! Help us set our non-negotiables. Strengthen us and give us courage to stay true to you and ourselves. Cover and prepare us for the discomfort and uncertainty. For we know that there is greater later. Allow my children, Elliott Brooks and Elese Brooks to see their importance and to stay true to themselves.

Prepare their minds for daily adversities. Keep their minds stayed on you! I ask in your son Jesus name, Amen!

Be blessed good people!

FAIL BIG

The other day, I was watching a college commencement speech that Denzel Washington was delivering to Dillard University students. One of the things he encouraged them to do is "Fail Big". His comments gave me a new perspective on failure. I will be the first to admit, I don't like failing at anything. Failure literally causes me anxiety. (Bubble guts and all! Lol) I work hard to perfect all that I do. So, when adversity comes I get so uncomfortable and my spirit is shaken. But you know what I am learning is that I need to EXPECT TO ENCOUNTER ADVERSITY. I have a habit of trying to find ways to circumvents difficulties. God's process for our lives is just that-his process. Sarah Young, in the book Jesus Calling states "Anticipate coming face to face with impossibilities: situations totally beyond your ability to handle. This awareness of your inadequacy is not something you should try to evade. It is precisely where I want you—the best place to encounter Me!" As I think about that, I think about what I tell my children- "Failure is not an option!" Well Elliott Brooks and Elese Brooks let Mommy be the 1st to apologize to you for telling you this. Failure is an option but it is how you fail!! FAIL BIG!!! Big enough to where your failure becomes your saving grace! Big enough where that failure becomes the gateway to your marvelous futures! Big enough the it makes your dreams your reality. FAIL BIG!

Father God, thank you today for Failure. Lord thank you for this word of wisdom today. I ask that you bless those who have allowed failure to consume them. Show them how to give you the glory and honor through their circumstances. Father open our hearts and minds to your plan for our lives. I ask today that my children Elliott and Elese see you in all that they do! Bless today Lord. I ask in your son Jesus name, Amen!

BE READY SET

As I sit here today on the plane headed back home, my mind is all over the place today-From my life, my children, my family and the current state of the world. It takes me back a few years when I was asked to speak for Women's month at my church. In preparation of that moment, I spent a lot of quiet time with God asking Him to remove Chana and allow his word to come free. As I reflected on my own life and what to share with the women, I realized that I had to be able to share my testimony. In order to do that, I needed to open up my private life, stories, and be vulnerable enough to show my genuineness. You see in order for use to help others, show love and give and gain respect, we need to Be Ready Set! As I began writing my speech, God said to me Be Ready Set! At that time, it meant preparing yourself for what God has in store for you, readying yourself for your blessing, and setting yourself up for success. Yeah, this is all still true. Today, Be Ready Set takes on a different meaning for me. Be just who God says you are. Ready yourself for the new chapters God will add to your book of life. Set yourself apart with higher expectations than you have ever had before. Be Ready Set!

Father God, today I come you asking for a Be Ready Set mindset! Lord prepare hearts and minds for what you have in store for us! Bless us to be just who you want us to be. Prepare us for our new chapters. Allow us to set higher expectations. Lord I ask that you let your will be done in our lives. Show us how to succeed and fail with dignity. Receive all the praise and honor. Today I ask you to allow my children Elese Brooks and Elliott Brooks to Be, Ready, Set! Be their own person, ready to receive all that you have for them and set to be different.

Allow them to accept your high expectations and be examples to others. I ask this in your son Jesus name, Amen! Be blessed good people!

SHUT UP!

Today is the 1st day of school for my babies. Traveling home from South Carolina yesterday, I was listening to a minister on the radio. His sermon was titled "Be Still and Know". I got to thinking about that. Sometimes we have to Shut Up! (Sounds bad, I know) Shut up that distraction to your life be still and know that He is. Shut up those distractions disguised as help, Shut up! Be still. God blesses in the stillness of his own voice. Quietness brings deliverance. Sometimes in our exuberance, we miss his voice. So today as children head back to school, encourage them to Shut up and focus on success.

Father God, thank you for this day. Bless children today. Keep their minds focused on you. For we know that you are the author and finisher of our faith. As Elese Brooks and Elliott Brooks start this school year, bring maturity, success, pride, and an intense dependence on you. Start right now Lord! Remove all hurt, harm or danger. Protect them. Keep them safe. I ask in your son Jesus name, Amen!

Be blessed good people!

SPLIT SECOND PRAYER

"Jesus!", "Help me Lord!", "Thank you Jesus!" Those are all thing we say throughout the day! Sometimes we say them silently and if you are like me sometimes we interject them in conversation. Those words are split second prayers. At that moment, they quickly connect us with God and remind us that he is just a short prayer away.

God, I thank you. Thank you for the connection. For always being right there. For never leaving us-being ever present. Lord as we start our day, give us wisdom to use the gift that you have given us. Allow us to pray before we speak, pray while we are listening, and not to respond to unnecessary things. Keep us poised and focused on you! In your son Jesus name, Amen!

Be blessed good people!

BECAUSE I KNOW THE GOD I SERVE

Sometimes we just need a reminder that God is BIGGER!!!! He is bigger than you, me, our circumstances, situations, shortcomings, and victories. If nothing else today, know that God's goodness and mercy is sufficient! Put that in your spirit today!

Lord, thank you for your goodness and mercy!!! I feel that in my spirit today! Share your blessings with others, God. Show it in the small stuff so that when you send your big blessings we are able to receive and embrace them with all of you! I ask in your son Jesus name, Amen!

Be blessed good people!

BLESSING IN SHARING

Life deals us all different hands. We may experience the same situations as others but we all perceive them differently. Today I was in a conversation with coworkers and my spirit was so blessed. God knows how to send reassurance just when you need it. I was feeling a little defeated last week. My soul and spirit was weak. I was questioning my abilities at work. You know sometimes when you work alone or remotely, you don't feel the support and often are encouraging yourself. But God!! In just listening to my team, I realized that I am not in this alone. They were feeling the same way. That was motivation enough to start my week off better than last week. You never know how just your conversation enlightens others. Your struggle could be just what others need.

God thank you for sending encouragement today! Lord teach us to lean on you and not on our own thoughts and actions. Remove uncertainty and weak thoughts. Replace those with Godly wisdom and strength. I ask this in your son Jesus name, Amen!

Be blessed good people!

"CLEANED-UP" SELF

I like very odd and different pieces of clothing, jewelry, and shoes. When I put those on I feel good. I feel set apart. Don't let have just set in Arlene HairQueen Banks chair- then I really feel fierce. My entire attitude is different. I have a new walk, talk and an uplifted spirit. That's the best "cleaned-up" version of myself! We all have that "cleaned-up" version. That's what we show the world. But what about the other you? The you not everyone gets to see. We all have a version of ourselves that we keep hidden from the world. We can't be vulnerable to everyone. God wants to know that version. He wants us to come to him with our broken pieces so that he can put us back together again. He knows you inside and out, so don't try to present a "cleaned-up" self to him! He ain't having it! Open yourself up to him so that you can truly live your "cleaned-up" self!

God, I come to you today vulnerable! Asking that you put all of our broken pieces back together. There are those who are really hurting and masking their pain and fears. Lord we don't know their hurt. But God I know that you are a God who can heal all hurt and pain. Fix the broken-hearted, weary, and worried. Show that you are the Master of this universe! I ask this in your son Jesus name, Amen!

Be blessed good people!

I'M BACK

I took time away from posting daily on social media because life got too busy, my children are out of school, my job consumed a lot of my time, etc... But just this morning, like a lightening bolt it hit me "You need that motivation more than anyone that reads it!" I will admit this week has been a real struggle for me. But God!! My prayer life is weak, my talks with God have lagged, and my quietness has grown louder and louder! The older I get the more I understand the importance to God in my life daily. Today is a new day and the best day to renew your relationship with God. God showed me today that he is always there.

Father God, I thank you. Thank you for never leaving me. Thank you for calming my spirit, for quieting my mind to focus on you and just being present. God, you know our struggles, fears, and desires. Bless us and fix what is broken in our lives. Give hope and peace. Show up in lives Lord. I ask this in your son Jesus name, Amen!

Be blessed good people!

HAPPY MOTHER'S DAY

Today is a day that is important not because of the material recognition that this day brings but what it symbolizes. As mothers and women, we represent a lot in this world. We are awesome wives, parents, sisters, aunts, and friends. We take on motherly roles. As someone once said, "we are the glue that keeps it together." I was watching Steve Harvey's tribute to his wife the other day (yes, I said Steve Harvey). He said that Marjorie allowed him to stop existing and begin living. She made his children comfortable, she made a place for his children to call home, she balanced out his life. She made happiness possible. Now that's a mother!!! Woman, we have been given that power by God. Genesis 2:18-25, states "18 Then the Lord God said it is not good for the man to be alone. I will make a helper who is just right for him. 19 So the Lord God formed from the ground all the wild animals and all the birds of the sky. He brought them to the man to see what he would call them, and the man chose a name for each one. 20 He gave names to all the livestock, all the birds of the sky, and all the wild animals. But still there was no helper just right for him. 21 So the Lord God caused the man to fall into a deep sleep. While the man slept, the Lord God took out one of the man's ribs and closed up the opening. 22 Then the Lord God made a woman from the rib, and he brought her to the man. 23 At last the man exclaimed. "This one is bone from my bone, and flesh from my flesh. She will be called 'woman,' because she was taken from 'man.' 24 This explains why a man leaves his father and mother and is joined to his wife, and the two are united into one. 25 Now the man and his wife were both naked, but they felt no shame."

So as we celebrate Mother's day, let it be known that it is not about the material items or about being the mother of your children. It is about what was divinely given to us. What we and only we can bring to this life. If you call yourself a woman, be about your Fathers business. Make happiness possible! Catch that! Make this year the year of DIFFERENT!

Be blessed good people!

CLOSER TO YOU

Travel for me in not just a part of work. It is also a time for me to become closer to the one I love the most- closer to the one who knows me better than anyone. The one that knows my faults and accepts me just so. The one who I can call on any time, any day, any hour and know that he will answer. The one who knows my journey and encourages me daily to walk in it. One thing for sure, he always has my back. Before I step on the plane, gives me sweet kisses and when I land he is always there with open arms. Being in his presence, makes me all warm and fuzzy! YES, the presence of GOD will do that for you!

Father God thank you for your reassuring presence. For I know I can count on you to show and give love. So today Lord, this is just for you! Thank you. Thank you! Thank you!! Thank you!!! Today God I ask that you bless my home and family! Lord I am sending up prayer request for Drew Thompson. Touch way down deep! HEAL from the top of his head to the soles of his feet. Lord I ask that you renew faith in you. Show all that you are all that we need. Today bless my children Elliott Brooks and Elese Brooks. Show them how to walk in your presence. I ask this in your son Jesus name, Amen! Make this year the year of DIFFERENT!

Be blessed good people!

LOVE

FB asks "What's on your mind? Well today, love is on my mind. Have you ever loved someone and couldn't share it? You struggle with those intimate thoughts all by yourself. The person you love knows but no one else does. Well, how do you think God feels when we don't acknowledge him? Today is deemed the day of love and intimacy to be shared with the one you love. What better day is it to express the love you have for God! Scream it from the rooftops- in the words of Erica Campbell "I love God. You don't love God, what's wrong with you?" God is waiting!!!! I love each and every one of you FB family! Enjoy your day today!

Father God, in the name of Jesus bring love, joy, and peace today! Someone needs to know they are loved today! Wrap your arms around them and show your unconditional love. Bless my children, Elliott Brooks_and Elese Brooks today as they start their day. Show them what it means to be loved! In your son Jesus name, Amen!

THE 17ᵀᴴ

Today we celebrate what would have been my youngest sister's Sharia's 35th birthday. As I sought out (as I always do) purpose for her life, I found this thought: "People who are associated with the number 17 often builds something substantial that will benefit many generations to come." So befitting. The light bulb moment- her purpose. When she passed, I struggled with the fact that people would forget her. That my children would forget her. Her friends wouldn't think about her. Our family wouldn't talk about her. That really had me feeling some kind of way. Then I realized, her purpose will be revealed. Oh, and it has. She has become my motivator, mentor, lean on, example, and push through. I was told by one of her friends DeArrius Howard "Just talk to her like she is right there in the room with you." I have full conversations with her. Lol. I now listen as my children Elliott Brooks and Elese Brooks share their thoughts and memories of her. I listen to our family share stories about her. I watch as her friends call or stop by my mom's to say "Mom, I was just thinking about her!" She has built something substantial that will last for generations to come! What are you building? Here's a thought: Take your birthdate (Mine is 15) and write down that number of goals, dreams, aspirations, or accomplishments you hope will affect generations to come. Celebrate as you complete each one. It only takes one to make a change. Make this year the year of DIFFERENT!

Father God, thank you. Thank you for legacy. I thank you for the people who surround me. Help me to build sustainability. Let my actions be a lamp for my children and family.

Show yourself in me. I thank you for the examples you have shown. Let others take heed. In your son Jesus name, Amen!

PS: Happy birthday Michelle Obama and Steve Harvey. Two people aspiring generations to come.

IMPOSSIBLE

I remember the 1st time I realized that God was able to do all that you ask him to do. I was in my early 20's and in what I know now to be a growing pain. I was praying hard for God to reveal to me his plan for my life not knowing he was walking me through it at that very moment. And then it hit me like a lightening bolt. It was like someone was in the room praying with me. God said "I am able! Trust the process!" I came out of that prayer, looking around and through my tiny apartment for the voice and the touch that was so real. But no one was there. I realized that it was God all the time. I began to thank him and praise him. You see when you get a taste of that Godly experience, it becomes impossible to thank him and praise him enough. I awoke this morning thinking on that memory and when I started my daily devotional, I realized that there is no amount of praise and thanks that I or you can give God that will be enough for all that he does for us! (Jesus Calling by Sarah Young is the truth. Get you a copy. It never gets old!) Today in all you do, recognize it is God!

Thank you Father God. I thank you for the possibilities. I thank you for making the impossible possible. You see so much in us that we cannot see. It amazes me when you see the potential and make it a reality. Lord how good that is!!! Father God as we start our journey today, free our hearts and minds of all impurities and open us up to the impossible. As my children Elliott Brooks and Elese Brooks start their day, show them how you move! Keep them protected and eyes on you. Encourage them to make good choices and decisions today. I ask this in your son Jesus name, Amen! Make this year the year of DIFFERENT!

Be bless good people!

SURRENDER

Have you ever wondered why? Why is work not going well, why your family is crazy, why you're at a stand-still, why you can't move forward, why is life so hard? I have had those exact moments. However, it wasn't until I surrendered and said God I trust you. I had to stand firm on all that had been instilled in me all my life, step out on faith, and say "God do you!" At these times, I reflect on the teaching at my childhood church 1st Centennial MBC and the guidance of Rev. Charles Jennings, the great teaching of my young adult church Friendship Baptist Church and late Rev. A Charles Ware and my current teachings of Cornerstone Institutional Baptist Church and the wonderfully anointed Dr. Brodie I. Johnson. I think about my family's expectations- the lessons that were taught by Karen Hughes, Rhonda Thompson, Doris Johnson, Grady Thompson, Rueben Johnson, Gerry Williams Thompson (foil wrapped egg sandwiches, lol) Debra Jennings-Thompson, and all my aunts and uncles (too many to name). Those experiences resonate in my soul and spirit. When I am feeling out of pocket, I have a repertoire of experiences that will get me back in pocket. However, during those vulnerable times, it is God that it seeks solace in. I turn to him and SURRENDER! Today is the day to learn to surrender all to God! Trust him!

Father God, today I pray this simple prayer asking for you to open your arms and allow your children to surrender to you! I ask this in your son Jesus name, Amen!

Surrender good people!

LORD, I TRUST YOU

There are times in our lives that we hurry to GOD for help. At other times, we rely on ourselves and other people. I challenge you today to learn a new habit!!!! In every situation, good or bad whisper "Lord, I trust you!" And watch what happens! You see, children of God, your faith should show up in all you say or do! It should seep into every situation in your life. Those 4 words are so powerful. They encourage you to surrender yourself to the grace and mercies of God! Trust me, you will experience a bit of serendipity.

Father God, I trust you today. I trust that you have laid out all life's circumstances and situation. I trust that you will block all evildoers, hatred, and all that is not of you. You, Father God have all the world in your hands. Touch those today who are struggling with trusting you. Show yourself worthy. Let our young people see you work! As Elliott Brooks and Elese Brooks start their day, remind them that it is you that they need to trust. Remind them to trust your process. Lift up the downtrodden, disappointed, and those who simple do not know you! I ask this in your son Jesus name, Amen! Make this year the year of DIFFERENT!

TRUST good people!

DIFFERENT

As we begin the new year, I ask how will I be different? Every year we make these unobtainable new year's resolutions that never come to pass. As I was doing my daily devotional today, readying my children Elliott Brooks and Elese Brooks to return to school and I to return to working from home, the word DIFFERENT just resonated with me. Instead of making broken promises, vow to be different. Have a different mindset, different actions, different responses, a different work ethic, different conversations (add God in your conversations), love differently, praise differently, give differently, show support and attention differently. Try somethings you have never tried before, go places you've never been before. Shed negativity and leave negative people in the wind!!!! I challenge you to leave the past behind and make the new year your new beginning, new start, and the year of "DIFFERENT"!!!!!!

Father God, thank you for a new year with new opportunities! Lord make me better. Allow me to live differently. All the heartache and disappointments of years past, remove it Lord. Replace it with a new joy and happiness. Continue to bless my family. Allow my children to be set apart, different. Show yourself in them. Let them be an example for others. As children return to school today, Lord be in the midst!!!! I ask these things in your son, Jesus name, Amen! Be DIFFERENT good people!!!

FOR GRANTED

So, I am a pretty private person. Unless you are my family or in my close circle of friends you would have never known that I had major surgery last week. Anyone who truly knows me, knows how difficult it is for me to sit still. But can I tell you, stillness is an awesome thing! This time recuperating is well spent for me. I have some time to praise, reflect, think, create, and plan. I realize the things I take for granted. Things like being able to walk, sit up, drive. The small stuff that we don't even notice each day. In this time, I am just resting in Him knowing that he is in control of all in my life! This year has had many blessings, joys, hurt and disappointments. I am so ready to start anew in!!!!

Father God, I truly thank you. Thank you for life and love. Thank you for the ability to love you!! Lord, my celebration of you is not just for the season but all year long!!! Bless my family, my children Elese Brooks and Elliott Brooks! Thank you for showing them you are real all year long. I ask this in your son Jesus name, Amen!

Blessings good people!

THIS MORNING IS
A NEW DAY!

A new day of change! We are living in different times. Know this, GOD IS IN CONTROL!!! As I had conversations this morning with my children, my response to their disappointment was for them to lean on their faith. God is in control! We are fortunate that we live in a country where we can invoke change. LET'S NOT FORGET THIS! I told my children to let this be a lesson to them and in 2020, (their 1st time voting) be that change. Regardless of your thoughts and feeling about this election, it would be a disgrace to last 8 years to let this moment ruin the plan God has for us! The decision has been made, now what? What are you going to do to make sure you don't feel this disappointment again? As I told my children, educate yourself, believe in your beliefs and DO NOT WAVIER!!! Stand for something. What do you stand for? If you don't stand for something, you will fall for anything! For those of you who did not vote, stop complaining and making comments about the candidates because you are part of the problem. YOU DID NOT EXERCISE THE RIGHT THAT OUR ANCESTORS FOUGHT LONG, HARD, AND SOME DIED FOR! It really bothers me when people have so much to say but can be about it!!!

God as we start this day, let me say thank you! Thank you for the lesson!! The lesson that you are still in control! Your plan will manifest itself! Show yourself GOD! I ask that you get into the hearts and minds of the Trump family and Republican party. Fill them with love, compassion, and understanding for your people! Remove disappointment and rally your people.

We will overcome! Bless my children Elliott Brooks and Elese Brooks. Remove despair and defeat and fill them with the mindset of hard work and determination. Lord we leave our country in very capable hands-YOURS!!! In your son Jesus name, Amen! Be blessed good people!

SPENDING TIME,
CHERISHING MEMORIES

I am so blessed to have wonderful examples of mothers. I woke up this morning feeling so overwhelming blessed. Yesterday, I was riding in the car with my mom Karen Hughes and we were just laughing and talking about everything. Last Friday, I was able to spend some true quality time with my 2nd mom Rhonda Thompson. We had breakfast together laughing and talking. It is these times that I cherish. The older I get the more I cherish those mother figures in my life. Debra Jennings-Thompson you have been my inspiration for so long! Denise Hall thank you for your love over the years.

It is my hope and prayer that I can be half of the mother and woman these ladies are. These ladies poured love and support into my young self, allowing me to grow into the woman I am today. Women set an example for the young ladies in your life. You never know how much you bring to someone's life. To all the women in my life, Thank you! Thank you for your time and investment in me. It is because of God and you that I can be my best self. Love you all!

Father God, thank you. Thank you for the love that you have placed in my life. Lord let me be the example that was set for me! Continue to allow me be the mother to my children Elliott Brooks and Elese Brooks that you have called me to be. Touch their lives just as these women have touched mine! In your son Jesus name, Amen!

Feeling soooooo super blessed! You too be blessed today good people!

INSTILLING

So, watching this video this morning, I cried at its beauty. I sat reflecting on those who inspires me. Growing up, I attended a small community Catholic school (St. Ann's). I was the best kept secret in my neighborhood. Not only because we were well educated there but because of the love, support, kindness, an overall general care and concern the faculty showed to each and every child there. The lessons I learned at St. Ann's went far beyond the classroom. They are so far embedded in the fiber of my being. Those lessons are being instilled into my children. A few years ago, while visiting home, I ran into my favorite teacher Sis. Donna Anthony! This experience touched my heart so much, that my sister and I followed her home and were greeted with open arms from the rest of the nuns. There we sat for hours laughing, talking and crying as we poured over memory after memory!!!!!! I credit these ladies for instilling their Godly presence in me! So, to Sis. Donna, Sis. Rose Mary (RIP), Sis. Linda, Sis. Mary Kay, Sis. Marie(RIP), Sis. Nancy, and Sis. Miriam, I salute you. Learn to inspire and sow into someone today! It will be the best gift you can give to the world!

Father God, I thank you today for the lessons. I thank you for the women of God who you brought forth to share the lesson. Walk through their lives and heart right now and tap dance these words of praise and thanksgiving! Let them continue to praise and honor you. For I know you are getting the Glory from the examples that these wonderful women exude. Thank you for allowing little old me to have great big blessings in my life. Continue to let your work show up in my life and my children Elliott Brooks and Elese Brooks. I ask this in your son Jesus name, Amen. Sow into someone today! Be blessed good people!

WATCH AND BE BLESSED

I love the way God drops things, words, songs, and people in my lap. Just when I need something to reassure me that things are just as they should be, God is always there and he uses his power in all ways, with anyone or anything. I recall right after Sharia passed, Elliott Brooks was 7 years old. We were riding in the car with my mom. Out of his mouth, out of nowhere he said "Grandma you are going to be ok! God needed an angel to watch over us. She is always around. She is here right now in this car. No need to be sad." At the very moment, we sat very quietly and let that message from God set in. You see what I have learned is God gives you just what you need when you need it! This morning I challenge you to seek him for what you need, want, and desire.

Father God, thank you! Thank you for your love and kindness. The love you have for us is far more precious that any material thing. I come today asking that you touch lives, hearts and souls today. Be a blessing in someone's life! Stop complaining spirits today. Bless my family and friends today. Show my children Elliott Brooks and Elese Brooks just how special they are. Drop love and kindness in their hearts and minds today. Continue to work in us as we work on ourselves. I ask this in your son Jesus name, Amen! Be blessed good people!

HAPPY SHARIA DAY!

Today 9 years ago, God gave my baby sister her wings. I never would have thought in a million years then that I would be without her. Yet, 9 years later here I am more grateful than ever. Grateful that God chose her to be my angel! What a beautiful gift. To speak of her and her passing as a gift even astonishes me because I miss her terribly but I now see God's plan. She being Sharia, her spirit, her determination, her motivation, her smile, her laughter, her hints of sarcasm, and her wisdom would all have been taken for granted if she would have stayed. She still motivates me to be my best self. I hear you baby girl every time I want a to give up- "Brooks, that's not cute! That's not hot!" You would say that I was your inspiration, but baby you will never know how much you inspire me!

Thank you God for this day. A day that reminds me every year that you still have the best in store for me! Thank you God for the life and legacy of Sharia Monique Webb, the angel you assigned to me! I pray today for my family, my mom and sisters. Mommy she is still present don't forget! I pray my children Elliott Brooks_and Elese Brooks remember that their Auntie LaLa loved them very much.

Thank you for allowing Diavonne Lawson and Toy Jackson-Williams to fill in the gap! Amen.

So today my tears are no longer tears of sorrow and hurt, but tears of joy and peace because I know she is watching! Be like butterflies today and fly in the beauty of the day. Be blessed good people!

SAFE

With all that is going on in the world today...I know that it is no one but God that keeps us safe!!!!! He is available right now for whatever you need and ask for.

God show up today and manifest your plan for my life, my children's lives Elliott Brooks and Elese Brooks, my family's lives. Show up in the world right now. Where those are weary, speak life Lord!!!!!! Lord I pray for peace and healing today! Bring insurmountable peace! Calm all life storms. Vindicate right now! Lord show the world right now that you have the last say so. I ask this in your son Jesus name, Amen!!!

Be safe in His arms today! Be blessed good people!

HOME TRAINING

" Good morning mommy I love u and God's going bless you and me today "...This is what I awoke to today from my Lovebug Elese Brooks.

Wow this touched me so. It feels good to know as a parent that the example you set forth is not in vain! My sole purpose in life is to ensure my children love God and can live the life that He wants for them. Yes, we get off course and off our God given path, but knowing God deep within and all that he can do will bring you back every time! Thank you Elese for making my day!

Father God thank you today for showing me the small things that mean soooooo much! God show us your favor today! Give little rays of sunshine today! As we continue today, allow us to appreciate all that we have. Bless my children Elliott Brooks and Elese Brooks as they walk in your way. Continue to watch over them. Lord you proved to me today that they are listening! I ask in your son Jesus name, Amen! Feeling blessed!

Good day good people!

COME REST

Have you ever awoken from a night's sleep and still felt exhausted? Mentally drained? Your mind is already focusing on that day's journey. Then listen closely- REST!!!!!! Listen to the sweet whispers of God saying REST! The best way to receive God's presence is to sit quietly and listen!!! Rest your mind from MAN!!! Get in commune with God! You know I travel all over this country for work. I have seen some great things, but the best thing about my travels, is when I can just sit in complete quietness! My mom use to get up early on Saturday mornings and sit in our sun porch, drinking her coffee. Sometimes she would read the newspaper. Sometimes she would just be. Then it would happen-We got up! She would say "You'll understand when your older." Oh mommy, I understand!!!!! The quietness!! Great things happen in the quietness!!! We gain our strength to go another further in the quietness! Cherish the quietness!!!!

Father God today I give you thanks for the quietness!!!!! Lord quiet our hearts, minds and souls today. Let us enter into great quietness with you! Quiet our mouths so that we can hear you. As we start our day's journey whisper "I am with you always." Bless my children Elliott Brooks and Elese Brooks today. Let youself shine in them today. Quiet their minds and seep in Lord. Get in their minds today guiding them to make good choices and decisions. Bless us as we start our day with only you on our minds. I ask this in your son Jesus name, Amen!

BE QUIET!!!!! Be blessed good people!

I USE THEM ALL

Yesterday, Min. Jenkins sermon was titled "Jesus Can Change Any Situation"! Yes, he can. She made a point that God gives us brand new mercies every day! I got to think about that- How special am I that I get new mercies EVERYDAY? I came to realize that I am not any more special than you. I remember some years ago Oprah gave away new cars to her audience. She said while pointing to each audience member "You get a car, you get a car, you get a car and you get a car!"They were all so happy because they received this special gift. Well today I say to you "You get brand new mercies, you get brand new mercies, your get brand new mercies, and you get brand new mercies!" Enjoy them. Use every one of them today because the good news is you get a BRAND-NEW SET tomorrow! Yes God!

Father God I thank you today for this set of mercies! I will be sure to use them all because I am coming with an expectant heart. Expecting a new set on tomorrow. Today, bless my children today Elliott Brooks and Elese Brooks today with the mercies you have assign them today. Lord ensure that they use them wisely. Lord let us not take you for granted. For those who doubt your grace and mercies, show yourself worthy. Lord as we start this work week, give us peace, calm any storms and remove any obstacle. I ask this in your son Jesus name, Amen!

New mercies good people!

BEHIND THE SCENES

We rise every day and take things for granted. Everyone does it consciously or unconsciously. We take for granted that all is well with our homes, jobs, families, and friends. Have you ever stopped and thought "What did God do or stop from happening so that I can have another day?" You see as we sleep, slumber, and go about our day, GOD never stops! He never stops blocking, fighting, and placing us just where we need to be. He is always behind the scenes making things just so. Today I challenge you to think on the goodness of the Lord and at that very moment just stop and thank God for working behind the scenes.

Father God, today I thank you. Thank you for your work behind the scenes to make all well. Lord, for those who take life, love, family, and friends for granted, widen their view. Show them how you move and manipulate. Today God I ask that you bless my children Elliott Brooks and Elese Brooks. Work behind the scenes in their life. Give them the wisdom to know that it is you that keeps them safe, loved, and protected from all hurt, harm and danger. Work behind the scenes. In your son Jesus name, Amen!

He's working behind the scenes! Be blessed good people!

SUSTAINING POWER

On yesterday, my pastor preached about sustaining power. He said that sometimes God just won't show up when you want him. He'll make you wait. What is God doing? He is building your sustaining power. Sustaining power will help you go a little further. It will make you see clearly and focus. It will make you grow up, mature, and seek God for all your needs. Sustaining power will calm storms and quite chaos. It will show you just who is in control. Today, pray and ask God for sustaining power.

Father God today, bless us with sustaining power. Power to see and know that it is you that is in control of every situation. You said in your word ask and we shall receive. I ask today that you step in and answer the prayers of your children. Someone needs you to release stress and turmoil in their life. Someone needs a shoulder to cry on. Someone wants to know you more. Show them today exactly who you are. I ask that you bless my children today Elliott Brooks and Elese Brooks. Give them sustaining power. Guide their paths to make good choices and decisions. We are listening Lord. I ask in your son Jesus name, Amen!

JESUS

Every time we login to FB to update our status, it asks "What's on your mind?" Well today good people, I have Jesus on my mind! Jesus- it is something about that name. I remember during the time of my younger sister Sharia's last days in the hospital, I was doing all I could to keep it together. One morning, I arrived at the hospital and no one was there visiting her but my mom and Sharia's manger from work. As soon as I walked into the family waiting area, I greeted them and then all I could do is call out the name JESUS!!!! Her manager began praising and praying for me. His name is so powerful. Another family was there and the wife walked by and said "You know who to call on. You're calling on the right one." No matter what you are going through or how difficult you think your situation is, JESUS brings peace in the mist of it all! The quickest way to calm a storm and redirect your mind is to whisper his name. He's listening!

Father God today, I ask that you bless us with your presence. As we whisper and call out to you, hear and answer us. Surround us with your peace and understanding. For that person who may feel forsaken or broken today, Lord restore belief in you today. Today bless my children- Elliott Brooks and Elese Brooks. For I know they know it is you that their help comes from. Remind them today! I ask that you continue to bless my family and friends. For those who don't know you, give them a little taste today! That little taste will keep them yearning for more! I ask this in your son JESUS name, Amen!!!!

Be bless good people!

REFOCUS

I tossed and turned most of the night. I woke up this morning with my spirit unsettled. I know when this happens, it's God trying to get my attention. It's him trying to make me aware that my spiritual tank is getting low. So, I got up and got into my quiet place (Boy, it is something about those quiet places). As I started reading my devotions, God ministered. He said "Trust me. Demonstrate your trust in me. I am training you to be aware of me at all times!" For me, that was a lightning bolt. Sometimes I just have to REFOCUS!! Refocus my priorities. Refocus my thoughts. Refocus my prayers. You see sometimes we get into our day to day, get overwhelmed and forget that God is still God and God all by Himself.

Lord, I thank you this morning!! I thank you for dropping the words of wisdom in my spirit today! Lord remind us throughout the day to trust you. Trust your training. Gently place your touches upon us each time we need to REFOCUS!!!! Dear God, I ask that you watch over my children (Elliott Brooks and Elese Brooks) today as they start their day! Keep your loving arms around them and refocus their minds on you. Protect and guide them. Bring peace that surpasses all understanding! I ask this in your son Jesus name, Amen!

REFOCUS good people! Be blessed today!

SOMETIMES WE JUST NEED TO BE REMINDED!

Father God, yes, it is you! You are God! Ruler of all the earth. Lord you're all knowing and a great deliverer. Deliver today! Yesterday's gone, tomorrow's not promised but TODAY Lord show us worthy. Release hurt, pain, sorrow and strife. Replace it with love, grace, mercy and peace. Touch many hearts today! I ask this in your son Jesus name, Amen.

Be blessed good people!

BARE MINIMUM
EXPECTATIONS AND
HIGH STANDARD

I t is ok to have expectations. Expectations for ourselves, in love and relationships, in school, in careers. At the very least we have bare minimum expectations. We expect our teachers to teach us because that's their job. We expect our jobs to pay us for the jobs that we do. We expect our mates to give and show love. But in order for these expectations to happen, we have to set a standard! In every situation you go into, go into it with an expecting spirit. Set a standard and let it be known. Not known just by the words you say but by the actions you set forth. In a relationship, you expect to show and receive love. Love is an action word. It is shown by your kind actions. By the comfort and respect you show. But your standards are to be a priority in your mate's life, be 1st, be totally respected, loved and protected. At work, your expectation is to be compensated for the work that you do. Your standard is a positive work ethic. This is shown by showing up, being on time, being accountable for your job duties, and seeing and being a part of the big picture. In school, your expectation is to learn. Your standards are shown when you participate and ask questions holding that teacher responsible for teaching you. Now that you know your expectations, set your standards high. Go over and beyond to make you mark on this world! So, when it is all said in done you can have God say, "Well done!"

Good morning Father God! Today I pray for expectations and high standards. Show us God high standards. Allow us to accept nothing less. For we are your children God and we know you expect only the best from us. Keep our minds set on you Lord! For when our minds are on you we can do anything but fail. I ask that you walk with us today God giving us that expecting spirit. Excepting that when we leave home we return to all is well! Show us God how to be more "Christ-like". Send us a praying spirit! Bless my children today Elliott Brooks and Elese Brooks today as they start the day with expectations and standards. God be with them as they assert themselves causing others to see the YOU in them. Guide and protect them! Help them to see their action are not only being seen by man but by you also. Guide their decision Lord. I ask this in your son Jesus name, Amen!

Expectations and High Standards today good people!

IT'S BACK ON!

Today is the 1st day of school for my babies... Yes, they are still my babies. As I sit and think, there are going to be many first today for lots of children and families. Pray today that God's covering keeps children safe.

Lord today is a day of first! I ask that you bless children today as they start on their way. Keep all hurt, harm, or danger from them. Open their hearts and minds to be focused on you and your will. Remove hatred and replace with love and peace. The devil can't steal our joy! Lord bless Elliott Brooks, Elese Brooks, and Xavier Logan_today! Show them that all is well. Guide them to make good choices and decisions! Protect them as only you can. I ask this in your son Jesus name, Amen!

Enjoy the day of 1st! Good day good people!

YES LORD

God is awesome! He can use anyone and everyone to prove his awesomeness! Don't take praise for granted! God moves during your praise. Today I challenge you to share your faith with someone else. You don't know whose life you are going to change, uplift, and win to Christ.

Lord, I thank you for small blessings. Small nudges that remind me that you can work all things out for our good! Thank you for the wisdom to recognize your small miracles. Rainbows, raindrops, rays of sunshine, quiet time with you, and all those other small reminders that show that you are real and with us every day. Lord today, I prayer that those who are struggling with giving you control, recognize your small blessings, remove self, and let you move in their life. Lord, I pray that my children Elliott Brooks and Elese Brooks continue to believe and trust in you and your small and mighty miracles. Reveal yourself today. I ask in your son Jesus name, Amen!

Be blessed good people!

EARLY FLIGHT

J ust landed in Phoenix. The start of a long work trip! Prayers up everybody!

Lord thank you for this day! Thank you for peace, prosperity wealth, comfort, security, plenty, and success. I am soooo grateful for all that you provide me with each day. Just enough!! Just enough to go further. Lord my desire is to live in my overflow so that my children, Elliott Brooks and Elese Brooks have much! Bless my family today. Lord show them that you are greater! Lord show them that you control circumstances and situations! Provide your miracles. Draw them nearer to YOU, Lord!! Extend your loving arms around them giving them peace that passes all understanding! Allow healing and forgiveness to prevail. Keep their mind stayed on you. Lord let YOUR will be done! I ask in your son Jesus name, Amen!

James 5:13-16 says: Is any among you afflicted? Let him pray. Is any merry? let him sing psalms. Is any sick among you? let him call for the elders of the church; and let them pray over him, anointing him with oil in the name of the Lord: And the prayer of faith shall save the sick, and the Lord shall raise him up; and if he has committed sins, they shall be forgiven him. Confess your faults one to another, and pray one for another, that ye may be healed. The effectual (successful in producing a desired or intended result; effective) fervent (having or displaying a passionate intensity) prayer of a righteous man availeth much. Pray with intensity and purpose today Fam! Love you much. Be blessed good people!

TIRED

What are we doing people? Where are we headed? Why is this happening? How do we end this cycle? When do we stop and make peace with ourselves? Peace starts with you. You make the decision on how you chose to act and react. Young black men, you have to stop giving people reasons to fear you! Pull your pants up, PUT GOD 1st, take education serious, PUT GOD 1st, stop using and selling drugs that cause the hateful spirits around you, PUT GOD 1st, get a job and earn an honest living, PUT GOD 1st, be great dads, PUT GOD 1st, respect yourself and women, PUT GOD 1st, gain an understanding of and appreciate the love, blood, sweat, and tears that were shed, PUT GOD 1st!! At the rate you are going, we have no future! PUT GOD 1st! I understand that PUTTING GOD 1st is a difficult task when you have so much negativity around you, but I promise you God is crying out for you to PUT GOD 1st! You are so use to quick, haphazard choices and solutions. Where is your patience, faith, hope and belief that if you PUT GOD 1st, he will show up and show out? Trust me when you think that you are in control, God says, "If you only knew. If you only knew what I was doing behind the scenes. I fixed this long before any of this happen. But you chose to take things into your own hands!! How did that work out for you?" TRUST the word of GOD! Proverbs 3: 5-6 says "Trust in the Lord with all thine heart; and lean not unto thine own understanding. In all thy ways acknowledge him, and he shall direct thy paths." You got to believe this!!! You have been trusting and believing what the world shows you and it hasn't worked. Try to PUT GOD 1st!!!!!

Father God, hearts are heavy today! Lord I ask that you send HOPE, FAITH, and BELIEF!! Belief that you are in control of this nation and world! Remove hatred. Lord we are praying, now we wait for you to do your mighty works!!! Show our young people (who are losing hope and faith) just how you handle evil doers. Lord I pray right now for my young people Elliott Brooks and Elese Brooks. I pray that they see the HOPE, FAITH, and BELIEF in their Dad and I each and every day! Continue to protect and shield them Lord! Every footstep Lord!!! I ask in your son Jesus name, Amen!

Have HOPE, FAITH, and BELIEF good people!

YES LORD!!! HE IS ABLE!

Good morning Lord! Thank you for this day!!! We are so blessed to see another day. God, I ask that you let your light shine bright today. Shine all over the world. Let everybody know that it is you that is able to do all things!!! Lord today as families start their journey for the holiday, get in cars, planes, trains, and buses, take hold of the wheel and guide them safely. Bless my family today. Continue to keep my children Elliott Brooks and Elese Brooks safe and focused on you. I ask in your son Jesus name, Amen!

Happy and Blessed 4th good people!

CONNECTING

When you are a parent that travels like I do, you connect with your children by any means necessary!!!! Social media is how young people connect to the world. This is how I connect and monitor my children when I am not in their presence. This means praying for them openly (even on FB) So for those of you who are wondering, My prayers are real and are to be encouraging to others- ESPECIALLY Elliott Brooks and Elese Brooks! So, don't get it twisted and read into my post trying to dig deeper because being obedient to God and being an example to my children is the only thing you will ever see. My children matter! Don't worry, grown people don't air their business on social media. If more of you prayed openly you wouldn't have to wonder about everyone else. Yes, I said it! Boom! Drop the mic! A mess!

Father God, in the name of Jesus, I ask that your word and my encouragement for others remain just that. Stop evil doers. Lord let you light continue to shine. Show up with peace and tranquility. I thank you God for the wisdom to know and put my children above all. Continue to bless and guide them. In your son Jesus name, Amen!

Now go tell that! Be blessed good people!

FATHERS

When I think of Father, I immediately think of my Dad-Grady Thompson!!! He is the true definition of what a father should be. He is a hard-working provider. That's what society says a father should be. My Daddy is so much more than that. He is a friend, counselor, jokester, listener, prayer partner, shoulder to lean on, and calm in a storm. As I have gotten older I realized just how humble he is. I have watched him over the years hold his peace and stand firm on the word of God!! Now that's a Father! Thank you Daddy for loving me unconditionally! I love you to pieces!!!'

Father God on this day I ask you to bless my Dad! Lord continue to keep him wise, humble and in your word. Show him that his work has not gone in vain. Allow him to see the fruits of his labor that extends generations!!! He is the head of our family and we all love him! Lord I ask that you bless all fathers today! In times when being a true father and daddy is rarely seen, show up in young men today. Sprinkle them with just a few drops of you Lord! Manifest in their lives. Show them that it is you that is in control! Lord I thank you that my children Elliott Brooks and Elese Brooks see great examples of what a man, father and daddy should be when they look at their dad, grandfather, and their uncles. Bless today God. I ask in your son Jesus name, Amen!

THE PERFECT GIFT

On June 10, 2000, my life was forever changed. God sent me the perfect gift! Elliott Brooks you are one of the two people my heart beats for. I am so grateful to be called your Mom. I am sooooooo very proud of the young man you have grown to be. Nothing makes me prouder than to see you as the well-mannered and respectable young man that you are. I would expect nothing less. To watch you over the years, has made my life so complete. Thank you for listening to and trusting God, your parents, and family to guide you through life. Our work is not done but you are off to a great start!!!! I love you to pieces!!!!!!!!

Father God, I thank you!!! I thank you for this special day. I am so full of emotions because I have a son that I can officially call a young man! I thank you for him!!! I thank you for his love, kindness, and respect. I thank you for his dreams, goals, and aspirations. Lord he could have easily chose the wrong path but it was your covering and our prayers that got him this far. Today Father God I ask that you continue to cover him. We are living in times that nothing but your grace and mercy keeps us. I am cashing in on some of my stored-up prayers for him!!!!! This is a day of a new beginning and new chapter in his life!!! Lord I ask that you continue to be those footprints under his feet. Guide and protect him! Keep his mind stayed on you! I ask this in your son Jesus name, Amen!

JUST TODAY

Yesterday, I had another wonderful time sitting with my Dad. One of my takeaways from this conversation was Just Today... If you know me well you know that I am a true Daddy's girl! And in that moment, it hit me like a lightning bolt "Just today!!!" So, what does that mean? So many times, we are so focused on the past or the future that we forget today!! Just enjoy today, the moment, the day, hour, minute, or second. Once those are gone, we can never get them back. These times are so precious to me! I was watching an interview with one of Mohammed Ali's daughters. She stated how when he was on the road, he would call, and they would record the conversation. Now she is so grateful to have those recordings to listen to. Most of us are not that lucky to have those precious memories recorded. But if we focus on "just today" they will be forever etched in our hearts and minds.

Father God, just today! I thank you for this day to make more just todays. Lord bless my family and friends. Let them know that your plan for them is already done. Just todays are a part of their plan. Father God, I know in the end, they will be just memories of just how good you are. Lord bless my children Elliott Brooks and Elese Brooks. Show them many just todays. We love you God. In your son Jesus name, Amen!

Make just today a blessed one! Be blessed good people!

HONOR

Today on this Memorial Day, I want to thank God for all those who served and lost their lives so that we can live! I remember growing up and my Dad would go to North or South Dakota for camp. As a young child, I always wondered what if he had to go and never returned? (The thought now still shakes me!) My mom teases me to this day about me waiting up as a child for my Daddy to come home so he and I can watch Mary Hartman. (Yes, I did go there. True 70's baby) My worry for my Dad's safety is what kept me up. We live today in a country where we are safe and free to live. It is because of God's covering over the men and women of our armed force that we can stand tall. So today, I salute you Daddy. Thank you for your unselfish service!

Good Morning Father God! Thank you for life, health and strength! Thank you for the gift of unselfish love. Lord, bless the men and women of our country who protect and serve us every day! Place your arms of protection around them and bring them home safe to their loved ones. Lord, we are living in times where no one but you can change the hatred of others. Seep into the hearts and minds of evil doers and those who cause hurt, harm or danger to others. Let them know that you have the last say. Lord, thank you for sparing my loved ones. I pray for the families who have lost loved ones to service. Let them know that the service was not in vain! Today I pray that my children Elliott Brooks and Elese Brooks understand the meaning of unselfish love. Show them the meaning of giving and giving unconditionally. I ask this in your son Jesus name, Amen!

Be blessed today good people!

Well Fam, I was watching a little one sing this morning! As she sings Erica Campbell's "I Luv God", I ask you if you love God! If not, what's wrong with you? God blesses us every day! Today let's just celebrate God, his son Jesus, and all that we have we been given!

Father God, we just love you. We praise you for just being magnificent, awesome, all powering, forgiving, and all knowing. Thank you God for all my blessings. Bless my family let them know I love them. Bless my children today Elese Brooks and Elliott Brooks! I love them to pieces! I ask this in your son Jesus name, Amen!

I love God. You don't love God, what's wrong with you? Be blessed good people!

FAVORED AND FOCUSED

I often hear people say, "I'm blessed and highly favored." Do they really believe that or have they fallen prey to the cliché'? When I think of being blessed and highly favored, I don't think of myself. I think of how blessed I am to be a blessing to others. When I think of being highly favored, I think of how God favored me to be a blessing to others. What has God favored you to do? Whatever he has blessed you to do, do it unselfishly. Bless without conditions. Father God, I thank you today. I thank you for your goals for my life. God, I ask you for strength and focus to endure my life journey. Remove stumbling blocks. Strengthen my focus on you! Father bless my children Elliott Brooks and Elese Brooks. Give them your favor for their life. I ask in your son Jesus name, Amen!

Now really "Be Blessed and Highly Favored" today good people!

POTENTIAL

When I was about 4 or 5 years old, I attended college with my Aunt Debra Jennings-Thompson. I can recall being in awe. As I sat there with her, watching her, I realized that I wanted to do this. It was in that moment that I recognized my potential. Potential is nothing more than small beginnings. Zechariah 4:10 states "Despise not the day of small beginnings". In order to meet your FULL potential, you have to maximize what God has given you. As I travel through life, I never forget that small beginning because it had catapulted me to things that I knew were possible. It is your time to find your Aunt Debbie. Your Aunt Debbie could be a person, place, thing, situation, or circumstance. Find something to carry YOU to your God given destiny. I challenge you now to do you! So many times, we focus on other people and problems but if we focus on God he will take us to our full potential! Philippians 4:13 says "I can do all things through Christ who strengthens me."

Father God today I thank you. Thank you for potential. Lord I ask that you bless us to recognize you and your growth in us. Lord place direction in our sight. Show us our small beginnings so that we can reach what you have for us. God I ask that you bless my children today Elliott Brooks and Elese Brooks. As the school year ends, let them reflect on their own growth. Use me Lord to show them their potential. I ask this in your son Jesus name, Amen! Be blessed today good people!

ASAP

As Soon As Possible. For years, I have used this term. When I want something done quickly, this is always a gentle reminder. I often use it with my family and friends. A good close friend told me that I can be impatient and I can be a lot to deal with. I know that God has taken great care in placing the right group of people in my life. Quite frankly, my friend is right!! You see for years (and even sometimes now) I wanted what I wanted when I wanted it. I was impulsive, somewhat demanding, and as my family says bossy! LOL. But I had a good heart!!! If I rocked with you, I rocked with you!!! I had high expectations (still do). But when you throw God in the mix, ASAP turns into Always Stop And Pray!!!!! So now my impulsiveness has turned to time with God. My impatience has turned into wait on God. My lot to deal with has turned into God's given plan. Oh, but my expectations, they have gotten higher. I have started expecting the unexpected! So today good people it is ok to ASAP because God is expecting it As Soon As Possible!

Father God thank you for this day. Lord I thank you for the peace that passes all understanding. I thank you for expectations. Lord thank you for showing me just what you can do!!! Today Father God, touch those who don't understand their God given plan. Make it plain for them. Show them how to pray and begin to expect answers to their prayers. Oh God when I pray, I am now in my expectant season!!!!! I expect your answers. I expect your blessings. I expect that you will calm any storm. I ask that you bless my children today Elliott Brooks and Elese Brooks. Place them in their expectant season. I ask this in your son Jesus name, Amen.

ASAP good people!!

CHARGED UP

Last night, it finally hit me- I was totally exhausted! I realized that I just needed sleep. I went to bed early and plugged in my phone to charge. I awoke today refreshed and well rested. But my phone was only half charged. I got to thinking, "Girl even your phone is half charged." Lol. You see that has been me for the last few months-HALF CHARGED!!!!! I was going and going until I completely wore myself out. When you are half anything, nothing gets done well. Now with my new found realization, l will have a new attitude and new priorities. So, let me give my answer now-NO!!!! No to aggravation, disappointment, unhappiness, stress, and definitely NO to other people's issues!!!! When I unplugged and plugged my phone back in, it rapidly began to charge. That's what we have to do- unplug and plug back in. By doing this, we become more focused on what's most important. I encourage you today to charge up!!! Unplug and plug back in.

Father God I thank you for this day. I thank you for the wisdom to know when a change and charge up is needed. I ask that you allow others to have the same wisdom to get charged up. Not for the world but so you get all the glory you deserve. We can only give you the glory when we are focused on you. Lord I ask that you strengthen those who are weak. Build them up and make them strong!! I ask today that you lay your hands on those who are suffering from misery and strive! Bless my children Elliott Brooks and Elese Brooks. As you said in your word "I can do all things through Christ that strengthens me!" Show them this truth! I ask this in your son Jesus name, Amen. Get charged up good people! Be blessed.

WONDERING

I often sit back and wonder what life would be like if... If I took a different path. If I didn't choose right. What if I chose wrong? I look at my life and I think "Girl your life could have been so different!" The what ifs often stops people from moving forward and prospering. My what ifs would have stopped me from my successes. Sometimes it is refreshing to stroll down memory lane. It makes you appreciate just how far you've come. I love the life God has given me. The good and the bad. My life was created just for me!! Has it been perfect? By all means NO!!!!!!! Would I change it? Absolutely NOT! Life is designed to build your character. Fear of it will keep you still! Don't live in regrets. Let God give you the life he planned for you! John 10:10 states "The thief cometh not, but for to steal, and to kill, and to destroy: I am come that they might have life, and that they might have it more abundantly." Make it your business to live abundantly today.

Father God today I thank you for life and life choices. I praise you for the wisdom to choose your path for my life. I receive your word today of abundant life. My choices may not have been your choices but God... You have seen me through some hard times but God... Lord I ask that you continue to share your abundant life with me, my family, my friends and my enemies. Lord teach them that you have a God given plan for their lives. They may deviate but God... Bless my children today Elliott Brooks and Elese Brooks as they walk today in their abundant life. Lord I ask this in your son Jesus name, Amen! Walk abundantly today good people!

A MERCY SEAT

God says that we need to create a mercy seat-a place where God can dwell amongst his people. A place where we can hear from God. As I sit here in my hotel room, it's quiet and I am creating my mercy seat. It only takes a little effort, time and dedication. Your relationship with God depends on quiet time. It is during these times that we can have personal conversations with the Master. If we just be still and quiet, God will always reveal his plan for us. He will direct our paths. Where is your mercy seat? Father God, thank you for today! Lord thank you for wisdom. Wisdom to know that I need time with you! Lord allow me to be quiet so that I can hear you! For I know being still grants me peace and understanding. Reveal plans for our lives. Thank you for your forgiving spirit. Forgive us today Lord. Make us righteous in your sight. Lord today I thank you for my babies Elliott Brooks and Elese Brooks. Every day with them gets sweeter and sweeter. I ask this in your son Jesus name, Amen!!! Find your mercy seat! You will be glad you did. Be Blessed good people!

MOTHERLY LOVE

As we celebrate mothers this weekend, I wanted to celebrate my mother Karen Hughes!!! I was excited to travel home to Buffalo this week. It wasn't just the fact that I got spend time with my Dad and my other mom Rhonda Thompson, but the quality time with my mom. We drove 13 hours creating memories. We talked, laughed, we sat in quiet. It is those times that I love because I don't just get to have her to myself, but I get to truly know her. I get to learn things that I can share with my children. I get to vent and cry and not be judged. I can share some of my most intimate thoughts and know that they stay right there. So, Mom today, I say thank you. Thank you for life, unconditional love, peace, friendship, hardship and the yummy, yummy, good you bring to my life. I am soooooooo blessed to have you in my life. You are my rock! I have been blessed to have many wonderful examples of great mothers. If I named all, I would be here for days. That is a blessing!!!!!! So today I celebrate mothers. I have a great one. How about you?

Father God thank you for my mothers Karen Hughes and Rhonda Thompson. Lord thank you for their wisdom and love for me!!! Lord let their light shine through me for my children. Lord for those who are motherless today, be the mother that they need. Show them special love that only a mother can. Today show my children Elliott Brooks and Elese Brooks my motherly love!!!! I ask this in your son Jesus name, Amen! Love your mothers today. You only get one! Be bless good people!

POSITIVITY VS.
NEGATIVITY

If we realized how powerful our thoughts are, we would never want to think a negative thought again. Mahatma Gandhi once stated: "Keep your thoughts positive because your thoughts become your words. Keep your words positive because your words become your behavior. Keep your behavior positive because your behavior becomes your habits. Keep your habits positive because your habits become your values. Keep your values positive because your values become your destiny!" You see a negative thinker sees the difficulty in every situation but one who thinks positively sees an opportunity in every difficulty. Having a negative mind will never bring you a positive life. No matter how positive you may be, remember, the devil is always around. He will send negativity your way just to see how positive you will stay. Proverbs 17:22 (MSG version) says "A cheerful disposition is good for your health; gloom and doom leave you bone-tired." (And I don't want to be tired!) It is my prayer that God removes all negative people, situations, and circumstances from around me. I choose positivity. What do you choose?

Father God, today I come to you asking for a positive change. Change that will shine as bright as your light. Lord show people that you and your mighty works can outshine the devil any day. Life is too short God and I know you can do all things. I pray that you renew people's minds. Give them new-ness. Refresh right now. Show them that whatever they are going through is not bigger than you!!! I pray for my children Elliott Brooks and Elese Brooks today. Pray that they see the positivity in the life that you have given them. Lord I ask this in your son Jesus name, Amen! Stay positive good people!

NEW VENTURES

Today is my last day at work. This was such a bitter sweet decision. As I sit here reflecting on my time at this job, I couldn't be prouder of myself for all that I have accomplished. I have learned a lot along the way. I built and established great friendships. I wrestled with this decision for quite some time. Do you know that when you pray and are obedient to God, he will reward you openly? In anything that you do, make sure it is done in decency and order. Once I stopped wrestling, God sent everything to me right on time. Sometime God has to move you out to take you higher. My new opportunity has really made me see my worth and purpose. You see I know this wasn't anybody's doing but God!!! Whatever you have been crying over or struggling with, sit back and watch God!! Yesterday at the Ship, Pastor Edward Jackson stated, "God says what I have for you is better than what you are crying over." I received that word. Let God!!!!

Father God, thank you for favor!!!! I thank you for opportunities. You are so worthy. God thank you for loving me and trusting me with your blessings. Lord when one area in my life is lacking, you always know how to lift me up and push me further! Bless my family today. My children Elliott Brooks and Elese Brooks mean the world to me. Everything I do is for them to see me give you the glory and praise. Thank you Father!!! I give you all the glory, honor and praise. In your son Jesus name, Amen! Be bless good people!!!

THE COMFORT
IN KNOWING

I t is always good to come home and be still! Every time I come home to Buffalo; I gain a better perspective on things in my life! I become more and more humble. I get the chance to seek comfort in just being with my Dad. There is nothing like Daddy. Most of our time together is just being in each other's presence. He can make me feel safe and ok without him uttering a word. Anyone that knows me knows that I am a true Daddy's girl. Mommies and Daddies always make things better. I love my parents.

Father God I thank you. Thank you for unconditional love. I thank you for life and how you hand pick every one that is placed in our lives. I thank you for my Dad Grady Thompson. Thank you for his unconditional love. I thank you for the gift of wholeness. Let us learn to walk in the things that you are manifesting and gifting in our lives. Father I know that later is greater. Let others believe this too. Some people have been shackled far too long!!! Dry tears today!!! Lose them Lord. You said John 8:36 "So if the Son sets you free, you will be free indeed." Free today Jesus!!! Lord I pray today that my children Elliott Brooks and Elese Brooks learn the meaning of your unconditional love. Show them today in my unconditional love for them. I love you God! I ask in your son Jesus name, Amen.

ELEVATION

The height to which something is risen. In order to be taken to the heights that God wants to take you, you have to shed some weight. Shed some habits, some people, material things and change your mindset. Will this be easy-NO!! But the reward you will receive in the end!!!!! God wants to bless us. However sometimes US hinders our own progress. It's time to accept your elevation!!!!

Father God, thank you for today. Lord let your people accept your gift of elevation!!! Move on their behalf today. Give them just a little glimpse of what you can do. It is my prayer that my family and friends experience your elevation. Remove those blocks that mean me no good. Please bless my children Elliott Brooks and Elese Brooks as they experience their own elevation today. I ask this in your son Jesus name, Amen! Be elevated today good people!

DRAWING NEAR

You see, the devil is always busy. When so much good and so many blessings come your way, the devil can't stand it. He will try to steal your joy. But God!!!!!!!!! This is when you draw near to God. God is enough to fight the devil off!!!!!! It is often said that you know who is really in your corner when trouble comes. How about when you are blessed, favored, and living in your overflow? Man can be a beast in these times as well. But hold on!!! Draw near and watch God work!!!!

Father God, I come today with thanksgiving. Thanking you for the devil being all up in our lives because I am always in awe at how swiftly you move to take him out!!! Show those who are battling the devil right now just what you can do!!! Bless those who feel defeated, broken, torn, mistreated, misused, and uneasy. Turn all that misery into joy, peace, victory, praise, wholeness, and most of all love for you!!! I ask that you bless my family and friends. I pray for my children Elliott Brooks and Elese Brooks today. I hope that they are drawing near to you. Let my life be an example to them. Keep them each and every time the devil gets busy. Watch over them today. I ask in your son Jesus name, Amen. Be blessed today good people. Encourage someone today!!!

WHAT IF

What if we do what is required from God? How will he bless us? Today is the day to start. Start trusting and believing he will do just what he said he would do. I am willing to believe. Are you? Good day Father God! Thank you for this day. You are already blessing this morning because I awoke and all was ok. My family is ok. My home is ok. Lord I just thank you. You see God, I trusted that you would make all well. Lord I pray today that the one who is struggling to trust and believe in you gets their breakthrough. I know you're real. Sometimes Lord you are so real I feel you sitting right next to me whispering I love you my child. I thank you for that presence. Peace comes with that. Understanding comes with that. Patience comes with that. That is a wonderful feeling of serenity. That's you Lord. I thank you for my personal relationship with you. Lord I pray that all of my family and friends get to experience you. Lord bless my children Elliott Brooks and Elese Brooks as they start their day. Just as I say to them every day "Make good choices and decisions today!", Lord I ask that you whisper the same. I love you God. I ask this prayer in your son Jesus name, Amen!

GONE TOO SOON

Yes, FBF we lost another one on yesterday. As I am listening to news reports, reading FB post, looking at Instagram, I keep seeing everyone say, "Gone too soon". What does that mean? Why do we do that? I am guilty as well. When my baby sister Sharia passed away I remember talk to my aunt Trina Battle telling her that I am not ready for this. And that was just it, I was not ready but God was ready!!!! You see we all have a God given plan for our lives. We may think that it is too soon but it is never too soon for God!!! Life is too short, so LIVE people LIVE!!!!!!!

Father God, thank you for this day!!! I am so excited to start your day!!! You gave me the privilege to see it so today God I choose to make it the best for you. I ask you to bless those who are hurting today. It is only a test, will you pass? Give them the wisdom to know that you and only you are in control. Bless my mind to stay focused on you and your daily tasks for me. Lord bless my family, children Elliott Brooks and Elese Brooks and friends. Let them know that someone prays for them daily. Protect their hearts, minds, and souls. I love you God. I ask in your son Jesus name, Amen!

ARE YOU MOVING FORWARD OR ARE YOU STANDING STILL?

Life is what you make it. You can't continue to be negative, complain, be ungrateful and think you are going to be blessed!!!!! You're missing your blessings people!!!!!!

Good morning Lord. Thank you for this day. Lord I ask you right now that you bless those who don't know you. I ask today that you remove all negative and complaining spirits from around me today. I welcome your positive energy. God, I ask that you fill hearts with joy and peace. Thank you for the small stuff. Thank you for the small blessings. Allow me today to be a blessing to someone else. Bless my children today Elliott Brooks and Elese Brooks. Give them peace and understanding today. Place your arms of protection around them. I ask in your son Jesus name, Amen!

ALL I NEED IS A TOUCH FROM YOUR

Brian Courtney Wilson wrote a song that says:
"All I need is a touch from you

No one else can do the things you do

Take the wrong in my life and make it right. Even me All I need lord Jesus

is a touch from you from my master and king all I need is a touch from you

Oh God Ho... God. Lord I'm standing in the need of prayer. When I call Lord, I know your there. Reach your hand down from heaven And pull me through

All I need is a single touch, a touch from the master oh god. All I ever need is a touch from you. If you touch me. I'll change my lose to win I will not lose I'll win, I win And live again New life I will You'll Take the wrong and make it right you'll make it alright you won't forsake me you'll touch me Jesus and hold on That's why I need your touch tonight your unchanging hand that will not waver even when I'm worked weak and worn out and fill with doubts about tomorrow cause I felt this pain yesterday cause I made so many mistakes I mean I stumbled and fell and I did not think I could ever be made over Cleaned up! But somehow I believe tonight That if you put your healing hands on me Every one of my sins Every one of my sins Will be washed away I wanna be made over I wanna be made over Everything I've ever needed Healing, peace, joy unspeakable joy Till you touch me lord Jesus Till you heal me lord Jesus Till I shine in the light of your glory One more time, I will, I will, I will All I've ever need is a touch from you

Even me. All I need, all I need, all I need. Don't be afraid join me at the alter God is here love is here."

What I have recognized in life is there is power touch. Watching this video this morning reminded me of experiencing God's touch in my own life. POWERFUL! God is real y'all!!!!!

Lord thank you for this day!!! You are awesome!! Today is a day of praise!!! We worship you God! We thank you Father God! Not asking for anything just wanting to glorify your name!!! You are almighty! Thank you for your movement in our lives!!! Thank you for saving who we thought couldn't be saved. Thank you for compassion. Thank you for comfort! You are merciful and full of grace!!! Thank you for shining and always being a bright shining light!!!! Lord you are so worthy!!!! Bless today, Amen!

WHAT IF WE RAN?

I looked at a video today of ducks running to the water and thought "What if we were this diligent for God?" We have a job to do for God. We should be making our enemy our footstools. God sets us free every morning. We spend all day dealing with the troubles of this world. Yet we can't wait to get up every day. We should hope that people are watching so that they can see the God in us.

Lord today, I come to you to with excitement and a spirit of expectancy. Expecting that you will remove troubles today and replace them with blessings and praise. Lord thank you for decisions. Indecisiveness doesn't feel good, but when you show up Lord, decisions are made and prayers are answered. I pray for those who lost love ones even in the last few hours! Someone did not see this day. Lord cover my children Elliott Brooks and Elese Brooks today as they start their daily journey. Stay in their ear Lord. Whisper to them so that they know you are standing near. Lord I just thank you for being you. I ask this in your son Jesus name, Amen!

KEEPING A
HUMBLE HEART

God rewards you openly when you keep a humble heart and spirit. Father God thank you for allowing me to be in your presence once again. Lord I just thank you and praise you. Lord keep my heart and mind stayed on you. For I know where my help and blessings come from. It is not man that blesses me. It is not man who keeps me safe and from all danger. It is not man that gives me the desires of my heart. It is not man who watches over my children and family. It is not man who constantly forgives me and gives me new reasons for life each day. It is not man who fills my heart with joy and peace. For it is you God!!!!! And I thank you for that. Lord I ask that you keep me humble in your blessing season so that I can be a blessing to someone else. Today watch over my family as they return to their various homes. Give them traveling mercies. Bless my babies Elliott Brooks and Elese Brooks today as they start a new day filled with brand new mercies and grace. I love you Lord and there is nothing you can do about it! In your son Jesus name, Amen!

BYOB... BRING YOUR OWN BURDENS

As we celebrated my Aunt Dottie's 70th birthday on yesterday, my heart was filled seeing all the family and generations together. Our ancestors would be so proud. All of their laid-up prayers answered.

Psalms 55:22 says "Cast thy burden upon the LORD, and he shall sustain thee: he shall never suffer the righteous to be moved."

Lord today as I come to you in prayer, I see your works. You did that, Lord!! I pray that burdens are lifted. Cares are cast to you. Show us that we are worth saving and worth dying for. Bless family generations. Move in someone's spirit right now. Stir up in the depths of their souls. Fresh anointing, brand new mercies, grace and favor!!! We love you Lord. I ask in your son Jesus name, Amen!!!!

THIS IS YOUR TIME

Lord I thank you for this day. Thank you for this time. I claim this shining moment in my life. I hope that my light is shining bright enough for others to see and catch on. Ride the Jesus training. I am overjoyed with the blessings I am receiving. Being obedient and trusting God brings about peace. Now Lord that I have agreed with and trusted you, a weight has been lifted. God, you get all the glory! I pray that others are blessed today. Lord I pray for those who doubt you. Continue to manifest your Lord! I ask this in your son Jesus name, Amen!

IN DUE SEASON

You will receive your rewards in due season. Father God thank you for your continuous favor. Today God I awoke with thanksgivings and a sense of calming. Immediately the devil tried to disturb me. Lord sometimes it can be difficult to focus on you with all of the worldly distractions. Oh, but when we do, you do mighty things. Lord I thank you for the process. Thank you for the path you laid out in front of me. Continue to direct my path. It may not be the path that I expected but God you make NO mistakes. For in due season...Lord I thank you for this season of change and transformation. I pray for all those who try and go against your plan. Show them it's not going to work. I pray for those who openly and secretly use and abuse our hearts and minds. Deliver them from their evil and unrighteous ways. Today God I pray for my children Elliott Brooks and Elese Brooks. I pray that they see the favor that you have bestowed upon my life. Continue to bless me to be the best that I can be for them. In the name of your son Jesus, Amen! Be blessed good people!!!

GOD SAYS YOUR WORK SHALL NOT GO UNNOTICED

A re you obedient?... Lord thank you for this day. I thank you Father God for the many miracles and blessings you bestow upon us. I stand in awe today at how swift your blessings come- how in an instant you change situations, lives, and souls. How crystal clear and plain you make things. God, you are awesome. Nothing you do ceases to amaze me. I thank you God for seeing my efforts to magnify you and give you all the glory. Lord you sure do know how to bless and bless accordingly. Today, Lord I ask that you do the same for others. Give them the desires of their heart. Heal broken hearts. Rebuke foolishness so that people can be blessed and see the true fruits of their labor. I know you can do it Lord because you have done it for me over and over and over. Time and time again!!!!!! I ask this in your son Jesus name, Amen!

THE DEVIL IS BUSY BUT GOD IS BUSIER

Lord God thank you for the blessings and favor that you are working out behind the scenes. It is awesome when you reveal things that we had no idea were coming our way!!! I know now what you have been speaking to me the last few weeks - Your blessings are in your praise, your purposeful delay, and Focus on you and all will fall in place. When we are obedient to you God, you really do show up and show out!!!!! Lord bless souls that are in much uncertainty today. Bless those who's words hurt others. Bless those who walk in their own way. Show them God just how marvelous, magnificent, forgiving, understanding, and in control you are!! I ask you this in your son Jesus name, Amen!!! Be blessed good people!!

WAITING ON GOD'S PURPOSEFUL DELAY

I woke up this morning thinking about all that God has done and will do in my life. But it was only in his timing. God's timing, gives us one of three answers — yes, no or wait. He will provide you exactly what you need.

Father God, I thank you for this day. Thank you for just being God. Lord you know the desires of my heart. As we are waiting on you Lord, clear our minds, strengthen our hearts. Lord I keep hearing you say to me "focus". Focus on you and all else will fall in place. I thank you for that word. God send your anointing this day. Send reassurance. Bless those who are not focused on you today. In your son, Jesus name, Amen!

NEW LIFE

In 1992, John P. Kee released a song "New Life". It says:

Oh what a change
Has come over me
My life has detoured
A life of misery
From darkness
You gave me light
All the wrong in my life
You came and made it right
He has given us new life.

Lord, as I look back over my life, I can thank you for where you have brought me from. We have all sinned and fallen short of the glory of you God but one thing for sure you truly have forgiven me and blessed me. You have given me new life. Through many losses I have sustained, it was you Father God that picked me up and dusted me off. I ask right now that the people who will receive this prayer, know that you will give them new life. Life throws us many unfortunate and unwanted situations, but God I know you to be the fixer. Fix people's minds, hearts, and souls. I ask that you show me today yet again just how wonderful you are. Peace... Father God today I come to you asking for peace. A peace that surpasses all understanding. Not only for me but for my family and friends. Father God I know that if only they could taste the peace that you have to offer, lives would be changed. I am waiting on you God expectantly. Today is a new day full of your grace, mercies and favor. Show up today! Bless hearts and minds. We love you Lord! In your son Jesus name, Amen.

Lord send a word today so that you stir up souls to give you the glory. I ask in your son Jesus name, Amen.

Be blessed good people!

GOD'S GOING TO TURN IT AROUND

L ord God I come to you today thanking you for the work you are doing in me. You know all that I was, am, and will be. I am so blessed to be your child. I give you all the praise. I heard a word from you saying it's all in your praise. So right now, God I praise you. I praise you for my circumstance good, bad or indifferent. I want to thank you for life and unconditional love! Speak right now Lord into my family, friends and enemies. You said in James 5:16 that "the effectual fervent prayer of a righteous man availeth much." Meaning a prayer that is showing great warmth, enthusiasm and intensity of spirit. Lord you know my heart. Today I pray that souls are saved so that they can taste and see how good you are. In Jesus name I pray, Amen.

BLESSED TO HAVE YOU

Father God thank you for another day! You are awesome!! As I am in your presence this morning, I am realizing that I am greatly blessed. Blessed because of all of your mighty works. You have seen me through good times and hard times. What's so awesome about your love God, is that it is unconditional. You said in your word that you want us to live life and live it more abundantly. I am ready Lord to live in my overflow. One thing I know is that you have surrounded me will the right people. So today God I ask you to bless those individuals abundantly. Give each of them the desires of their heart. Unveil yourself to them. Show them what you've shown me. Thank you God for your unconditional love. Bless right now! In the name of Jesus, Amen.

THE MOMENT YOU REALIZE THAT GOD IS IN CONTROL

It is a beautiful thing when we can allow God to control our every move. Although beautiful, it is very difficult. We live in the flesh and Father God we thank you for another day. Thank you for a day filled with all of your grace and mercies. You said in your word that if we ask in your name we will receive. I am asking right now Lord to bless my children, my family and my friends. Lord show up and show out today. Let the world know that you are God and God all by yourself. You don't need any help to be magnificent. You got that all tied up. Thank you Lord for your arms of protection as I travel this country. It is nobody but you that covers me. Lord I thank you for blessings seen and unseen because I know that you have great plans for me. I am blessed just because you are you and I know you make no mistakes. I ask that whatever we prayer for, you give us the strength and courage to leave it your feet to answer. Lord cover my children Elese Brooks and Elliott Brooks as they take on today's journey. I love you Lord. I ask this in your son Jesus name. Amen.

MY SPECIAL GIFT

As people share their Thanksgiving and holiday wish, I think about where I was 19 years ago. I was embarking on a 4-day journey that would give me one of my prize possessions. She was not supposed to be born until her daddy's birthday in January. I ate myself so full that I went into labor early. So, there I was with Elliott Brooks at home with labor pains. Their dad was in Buffalo visiting my dad Grady Thompson. Every time a pain would hit Two, with his little self would rub my back. I called my mom and told her that I think I need to go get checked at the hospital. That was the beginning of one of the scariest times in my life. I thought, God this is truly in your hands. After 4 days of labor, she arrived 24 minutes after her Daddy arrived at the hospital. She was waiting for him. God is so awesome! Two months premature and no major health issues or concerns! To see her now, you would never know how fragile her 1st six months of life were. Elese Brooks, Mommy loves you to the moon and back. Thank you for all that you bring to my life- unconditional love, patience, humor, admiration. You don't know how much you push me to be great. Thank you for the beautiful young lady you are becoming!!! Father God, thank you! Thank for Elese! Lord continue to manifest in her life! Show her worth and value! Please provide her the desires of her heart. All that she was, is and aspires to be is in your hands Lord. Bless her now and forever. In your son Jesus name, Amen! I love you Leesee Pooh!